IMAGES
of America

GRAND ESTATES
OF GROSSE POINTE

15530 WINDMILL POINTE. 15530 Windmill Pointe was completed in 1929 by a leading architectural firm, Smith, Hinchman & Grylls, for Hal Smith, a partner in the prominent Detroit law firm Beaumont, Smith, and Harris. The grand 14,547-square-foot Colonial Revival home is situated on a 1.9-acre lot overlooking the lake. The magnificent 32-by-45-square-foot library features a beautiful cathedral ceiling and oak paneling. (Courtesy of Higbie Maxon Agney.)

ON THE COVER: LAKE TERRACE, RESIDENCE OF JOHN S. NEWBERRY (AFTER THE REMODEL IN THE EARLY 1890s). This photograph, taken between 1890 and 1901, shows the residence of John S. Newberry and his wife, Helen P. Newberry. Completed in 1875, the three-story summer cottage was designed by Gordon W. Lloyd. After Mr. Newberry passed in 1887, Mrs. Newberry remodeled the cottage in the early 1890s. It was demolished around 1910. (Courtesy of the Library of Congress, LC-D4-12789 [P&P].)

IMAGES
of America

GRAND ESTATES
OF GROSSE POINTE

Katie Doelle
Foreword by Kay Agney

ARCADIA
PUBLISHING

Published by Arcadia Publishing
Charleston, South Carolina

Printed in the United States of America

Library of Congress Control Number: 2019952929

For all general information, please contact Arcadia Publishing:
Telephone 843-853-2070
Fax 843-853-0044
E-mail sales@arcadiapublishing.com
For customer service and orders:
Toll-Free 1-888-313-2665

Visit us on the Internet at www.arcadiapublishing.com

Dedicated to my loving husband, William,
the man with a thousand books . . .
and now he has one by his wife

CONTENTS

FOREWORD

Since my first drive down Lake Shore Road in the late 1970s, I have been fascinated by the beauty and history of this great community. Originally settled by French farmers, the beauty of the area gave way to wealthy Detroit industrialists establishing summer homes along the lake and eventually building grand estates overlooking Lake St. Clair. As the population grew, more modest homes and neighborhoods sprang up, and today, we enjoy a very vibrant community steeped in tradition and history.

I had the great fortune to begin my career at Higbie Maxon REALTORS®, where owner Hugo S. Higbie was passionate about Grosse Pointe and preserving its storied past. Hugo was able to preserve that history through his firsthand account of life in Grosse Pointe in his monthly "Hugo's Corner" articles and with the archive of detailed historical data preserved at Higbie Maxon Agney REALTORS®. We felt this information needed to be shared and not just stored in perpetuity, so we enlisted the help of Katie Doelle to write a weekly blog about the architectural history of Grosse Pointe using the information we had collected. The blog has been a great success, due in no small part to Katie's thorough attention to detail. She is a talented writer, and her book brings the history of the Grosse Pointes, the families, and their homes to life. In each chapter, readers will meet the architects and their clients who gifted Grosse Pointe with so many architecturally interesting homes. The last chapter is dedicated to the many grand estates that were torn down over the years. Thankfully, they have been preserved in pictures. This book will remind every reader what a treasure we share in Grosse Pointe.

Enjoy!

—Kay Agney

ACKNOWLEDGMENTS

This book would not have been possible without the generosity and support of Kay Agney—architectural enthusiast and owner and broker of historic Grosse Pointe REALTOR® Higbie Maxon Agney—who granted me access to the company's vast collection of files and images.

A big thank-you goes to Suzy Berschback for recommending me to Arcadia Publishing, my good friend Diana Greenwood for her editing skills, and to my very patient husband, William, who scanned all the images.

I would also like to thank Belinda Krencicki and Ashley Stevens at the Edsel and Eleanor Ford Estate, the Kornmeier family, Charles Burke and Jessi Kaminski at the War Memorial, the Junior League of Detroit, and the Library of Congress.

Most of the images come from a limited number of sources. Instead of writing the names of the organizations each time, the names have been abbreviated as follows: Higbie Maxon Agney (HMA); the Library of Congress (LOC); Honest Opinion Design (HOD), the Junior League of Detroit (JLD), and the War Memorial (TWM.)

The term *Grosse Pointe* (GP) is used to refer to the entire area, referencing all five adjacent individual cities—Grosse Pointe, Grosse Pointe Farms, Grosse Pointe Park, Grosse Pointe Shores, and Grosse Pointe Woods.

INTRODUCTION

The earliest inhabitants of Grosse Pointe can be traced back to the mid-18th century, when French farmers occupied ribbon farms on the shores of Lake St. Clair. Since then, Grosse Pointe, sometimes called "The Pointes" or simply "GP" by its residents, has come a long way. The once rural farming community, located on marshland and notoriously difficult to reach, became home to some of the most prestigious residences in the country.

The transformation of Grosse Pointe, economically, demographically, and architecturally, has come in a series of stages. In the mid-19th century, Grosse Pointe was primarily woods and farms, and any clearings that were located on the waterfront were devoted to orchards. During the latter parts of the century, lumbermen began to clear the wooded areas, and wealthy Detroit businessmen started to buy land on the lakefront to build summer cottages; Grosse Pointe, by now, was becoming a popular summer resort. The majority of the summer homes were typical of the Gothic Revival and Queen Anne architectural styles of that period. They were located on the edge of the lake, with well-manicured lawns and elegant flower gardens.

Toward the end of the 19th century, the interurban railway was opened, linking Detroit to Mount Clemens via Grosse Pointe. The railway, coupled with vast improvements to the roads and the dawn of the automobile, made Grosse Pointe far more accessible and paved the way for the first year-round homes to be constructed. Villages were organized, and subdivisions were created. Many of the early summer cottages were later demolished to make way for large mansions with formal landscaped gardens.

As the desire to move to the suburbs began to gain momentum, some of the finest architects in the nation were hired to design luxurious homes. These talented designers brought with them innovative ideas and the latest architectural trends to create majestic Arts and Crafts, Italian Renaissance, Colonial Revival, and English-inspired homes. With those designers came nationally recognized landscape architects who created extensive grounds.

After World War I came the Roaring Twenties. It was a time of prosperity, change, and growth. From 1920 to 1930, the population in Grosse Pointe rose 321.8 percent—from 5,088 in 1920 to 21,462 in 1930. By 1940, the population reached 29,648. It was also a golden era of architectural significance, development, and transformation, nationally and across Metro Detroit, in particular Grosse Pointe. With the population growing, many of the Grosse Pointe cities were in a significant period of expansion. Grosse Pointe Farms in particular was witnessing a dramatic change to the architectural scene, thanks, in part, to the prestigious architects working in the community and also to the some of the evolving design trends that were coming from Europe. This period also witnessed major development in Grosse Pointe Park, especially the area known as Windmill Pointe. During the 1920s, Windmill Pointe was at the height of popularity and became a much sought after area.

Along with the construction of the grand estates came schools, modern city services, hospitals, clubs, and churches. By the 1930s, a core group of prominent architects was transforming the style of homes that were built throughout the community. This not only led to a consistent look and feel but also influenced the work of lesser-known architects. The 1930s also witnessed the effects of the Great Depression, the desire for smaller homes, a migration from the more formal Tudor and Georgian residences, and new architectural trends from both national and international sources. Many of the noted local architects evolved their styles to accommodate the growing trend for Art Deco, Regency, and International type homes, while several of these key designers were also hired to transform some of the existing large mansions into more suitable spaces for modern living.

During the 1940s, new architectural neighbors began to arrive. The more formal homes were joined by numerous Mid-Century Modern masterpieces, while some of the older, larger, and traditional grand mansions, commissioned by the auto barons during the early-20th-century industrial boom, were starting to disappear. As the original owners began to move or pass away, the realization of the hard work and expense to maintain these larger homes was beginning to be understood. Many were sold, and then razed, to make way for new subdivisions, which, in part, were named after the early French farmers or after the prominent families who once owned large estates in the community. Grosse Pointe Woods in particular was in an intense period of growth, so much so that there became a shortage of street names for the new subdivisions. One of the area's more prominent developers solved the problem by deciding to name some of the streets after the "hardworking people in his office."

Grosse Pointe, however, is not without controversy, and there has always been aversion to change. During the 1950s and 1960s, some of the finest estates in the country were demolished to make way for new subdivisions. Between the mid-1950s and mid-1970s, a new band of architects was hired to create multiple homes across the community, as were local recognized builders who specialized in developing subdivisions within the area.

As Grosse Pointe continues to evolve, numerous buildings have been awarded prestigious designations—listed in the National Register of Historic Places, designated as a Michigan State Historic Site, or awarded a Bronze Historic Plaque by the Grosse Pointe Historical Society in recognition of its historical or architectural value to the community.

Today, Grosse Pointe is awash with renowned families, natural beauty, historical architecture, and many grand estates.

One

THE EARLY YEARS FROM 1890 TO 1920

In the mid-18th century, many of the French settlers who resided in Detroit left the city and moved to Grosse Pointe to join the already established French families who owned much of the farmland in the area. Beginning in the 1850s, the community, located on marshland and notoriously difficult to reach, began to transition into a popular summer retreat for wealthy Detroit families.

The majority of the summer homes were located on the edge of the lake. They were typical of the Gothic Revival and Queen Anne architectural styles of that period, with well-manicured lawns and elegant flower gardens. A few "turn of the century" summer cottages can still be found on Lake Shore Road today.

During the very early 20th century, some of the first year-round homes began to be built, thanks in part to Lake Shore Road becoming a paved road, the dawn of the automobile, and the desire for many of Detroit's wealthy residents to move out of the city. One of the first instances of subdividing land, to sell to Detroiters, came in 1906 when an orchard was removed and McKinley Place was subdivided from Lake Shore Road to Grosse Pointe Boulevard. This division helped signal the start of the demolition of many of the early summer cottages to make way for the large mansions with their formal landscaped gardens.

As the desire to move to the suburbs began to gain momentum, some of the finest architects in the nation were hired to create these luxurious homes, including Albert Kahn, William Buck Stratton, Louis Kamper, and George D. Mason. These talented designers brought with them innovative ideas and the latest architectural styles and trends to create majestic Arts and Crafts, Italian Renaissance, Colonial Revival, and English-inspired homes.

By 1920, the shores, park, farms, and the city had been incorporated as independent villages, and Grosse Pointe was well on the way to becoming a thriving and ever expanding community.

16109 East Jefferson Avenue. This property lays claim to being the oldest brick house in the Grosse Pointe communities. Henry Seitz built the two-story Colonial-style home in 1849 for a prosperous English farmer—William Buck—who had purchased the land in 1845. In 1901, Henry Russel, an attorney and businessman, purchased the house. Because Russel spent most of his time at his residence in Detroit, in 1912 he gifted the house to his daughter Helen and her new husband, Harold F. Wardwell. That same year, renowned local architect William Buck Stratton was hired to make extensive renovations to the home. Helen Wardwell resided in the home until her death in 1976. Wardwell House is listed in the Michigan State Register of Historic Sites. (Courtesy of LOC, HABS MICH, 82-GROSP,1-.)

300 LINCOLN ROAD. Detroit-based architect George E. Graves designed this Colonial-inspired property in 1915 for Olive and Edwin Hewitt Brown, a prominent family in the community. Olive served with the rank of major in the canteen of the Army and Navy Club of Detroit. A 1915 article in *Home and Garden* magazine (Volume 27) described the floor plan as "being divided into distinctive units." (Courtesy of HMA.)

330 LINCOLN ROAD. Completed in 1911, this early Colonial-inspired home was designed by George W. Graves for Cameron B. Waterman, a lawyer and inventor of the outboard motor. The classically designed symmetrical home was increased in size several years later with the addition of a two-story Tudor-inspired extension at the rear of the home. (Courtesy of HMA.)

32 LAKE SHORE DRIVE. Completed in 1910, the residence at 32 Lake Shore Drive, The Moorings, was originally the home of Russell A. Alger Jr. and his wife, Marion Alger. Nationally recognized architect Charles Adam Platt, who was inspired by Italian Renaissance architecture, designed it. Set on 4.5 acres, the property was one of the finest country estates on Lake Shore Drive, with magnificent views of the lake. After Russell Alger passed in 1930, Marion Alger donated the family home to the Detroit Institute of Arts in 1936 to serve as a branch of the museum until 1942. In 1949, Marion Alger donated the house to the Grosse Pointe War Memorial Association in memory of a grandson who was killed in World War II. Today, the War Memorial is a center for educational and charitable purposes as well as being a memorial to the Grosse Pointers who served their country. (Both, courtesy of TWM.)

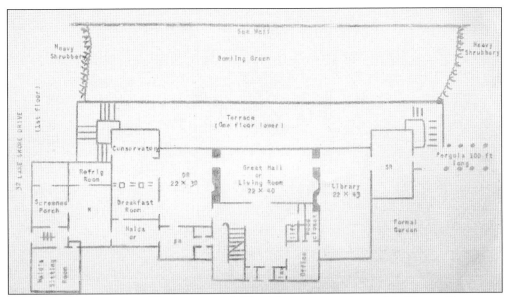

32 Lake Shore Drive. The interior of The Moorings was beautiful. The ceilings were particularly striking; the walls in the dining room and the billiard room were paneled in wood, imported from England. The nine fireplaces included one in carved wood and two in carved stone, imported from Italy. A hand-operated elevator ran from the basement to the second floor. The floor plan is the original layout of the first floor, prior to The Moorings becoming the War Memorial. (Courtesy of HMA.)

99 Lothrop Road. Renowned architect Charles A. Platt designed a large 8,000-square-foot stately manor for Allen F. Edwards, an original board member of Chrysler. Platt, a self-trained architect and considered one of America's more influential landscape designers, commissioned landscape architect Ellen Biddle Shipman to design the formal garden. The pair had already collaborated on a previous project at 32 Lake Shore Road in 1910. (Courtesy of HMA.)

15

COUNTRY CLUB OF DETROIT, 1890. With a growing residential community, the organization of the Grosse Pointe Club hired architect William E. Brown to design a clubhouse. Completed in 1886, the building was located on the shores of Lake St. Clair on a scenic seven-acre site. Constructed of wood on a brick foundation, the large circular tower, with its giant conical roof, provided great views of the lake and the grounds. Two years after completion, the clubhouse was forced to close due to membership issues. Despite the clubhouse being popular with local residents, the poorly maintained roads from Detroit to Grosse Pointe made access to the club difficult. In the late 1880s, transport links with Detroit were vastly improved and the club became more accessible. It reopened in 1897, under the name of the Country Club of Detroit. (Courtesy of LOC, LC-D4-10431 [P&P].)

THE PARLOR AND RECEPTION HALL IN THE COUNTRY CLUB, 1890 AND 1900. The total cost to complete the country club—the building, furniture, and grounds—was around $50,000 (around $1.2 million today). The clubhouse was created to accommodate 300 members when full. Each member was expected to pay an annual assessment fee for the maintenance of the club, along with an initiation fee of $150 (close to $4,000 today). The main hall was around 15 square feet wide; it extended to the rear of the building and a 16-foot by 30-foot loggia that faced the lake. A particularly striking feature to the clubhouse was the 16-foot-wide veranda, which stretched 322 feet around the north, east, and south sides to provide a perfect place for lounging during the summer months. (Both, courtesy of LOC; above, LC-D4-12455 [P&P]; below, LC-D4-12454 [P&P].)

COUNTRY CLUB OF DETROIT, 1910. To accommodate the growing population, a larger, more modern clubhouse was required for the Country Club of Detroit. Albert Kahn was hired to design a state-of-the-art brick building to be located on part of the original site. The new four-story clubhouse was completed in 1907 and featured many modern components, including a large, full-length, glass-enclosed veranda. The original clubhouse, which had been completed in 1886, was later demolished. Meanwhile, membership at the club continued to grow. In 1924, the Kahn-designed clubhouse was demolished, and a new clubhouse was built on a new site (220 Country Club Drive), where it stands today. (Both, courtesy of LOC; above, LC-D4-70328 [P&P]; below, LC-D4-72779 [P&P].)

THE ARTS AND CRAFTS MOVEMENT. Toward the end of the 19th century, the Arts and Crafts movement had begun to emerge in Detroit and across the United States. Already popular in Europe, the trend captured the imagination of many prominent designers in Detroit such as Albert Kahn and William B. Stratton. Both men were huge advocates of the movement and were instrumental in staging Detroit's first annual Arts and Crafts exhibition in 1904. Frank E. Hill designed 560 Cadieux Road (above) in 1911 (the height of the movement's popularity) for Harold Prell Breitenbach. Another early Arts and Crafts–inspired home is 319 Lincoln Road (below), designed by Norval Wardrop for Harold D. Baker in 1912. The Arts and Crafts movement remained popular until the 1930s. (Both, courtesy of HMA.)

55 TONNANCOUR PLACE. The street of Tonnancour Place was originally part of the Theodore Parsons Hall estate—a 63-acre lot that contained Hall's summer residence. After Hall's death in 1909, the lot was subdivided, around 1914. Hall's daughter and her husband, Frederick Fuger, a captain in the US Army, commissioned Washington, DC–based architect Edward W. Donn Jr. to design 55 Tonnancour Place, a Georgian Revival–inspired home completed in 1914. (Courtesy of HMA.)

59 LAKE SHORE DRIVE. The Sherrard House is one of the last few remaining 19th-century homes in Grosse Pointe. Designed by the prestigious firm of Mason & Rice, it was commissioned in 1892 by Joseph Berry for his eldest daughter, Charlotte, and her husband, Henry Sherrard, cofounder of Detroit University School (now University Liggett). The 4,400-square-foot house is constructed from red-brown sandstone with cedar shingles. It is listed in the Michigan State Register of Historic Sites. (Courtesy of HOD.)

LAKE TERRACE, RESIDENCES OF SEN. JAMES MCMILLAN (ABOVE) AND JOHN S. NEWBERRY (BELOW). Toward the end of the 19th century, James McMillan and John S. Newberry were pivotal in developing the residential growth of Grosse Pointe and the industrial growth of Detroit. In 1875, having purchased numerous French strip farms in the community, they commissioned Gordon W. Lloyd to create nearly identical three-story summer cottages named Lake Terrace. Built in the same architectural style, the summer cottages were the first of their kind in Grosse Pointe and proved to be influential in turning Grosse Pointe into an exclusive summer venue for Detroit's wealthy families. The property, part owned by Alfred E. Brush, included a long dock where Newberry moored his steam yacht *Truant*. Both properties were demolished around 1910. (Both, courtesy of LOC; above, LC-D4-12788 [P&P]; below, LC-D4-12789 [P&P].)

372 Lakeland Street and 17330 Maumee Avenue. Completed in 1909 for John M. Dwyer, joint founder of one of Detroit's largest stove manufacturing companies, this 12,000-square-foot residence is one of the finest Georgian homes in the community. George Hunt Ingraham designed it. The estate was located on a huge lot and included a carriage house, guesthouse, and a horse stable, all of which were surrounded by a lush formal garden. The house originally sat across from what is now Lakeland Street; however, at some point, the land was subdivided and the immense mansion was moved approximately 100 feet and rotated 90 degrees to face Lakeland Street. The original carriage house is now 17330 Maumee Avenue (below), and the guesthouse became 382 Lakeland Street. (Both, courtesy of HOD.)

16004 EAST JEFFERSON AVENUE. This English Tudor–style residence was completed in 1907 by the Detroit-based firm of Mildner & Eisen for Dr. Herman Kreit. The house was located on a half-acre lot, surrounded by an abundance of trees, including lilac and ancient pear. Following his retirement as a dentist in 1908, Dr. Kreit became president of the village of Grosse Pointe Park. The Kreit family owned the property until 1969. (Courtesy of HMA.)

41 PROVENCAL ROAD. In 1906, Lewis H. Jones commissioned Albert Kahn to design a grand Tudor Revival home in Indian Village. The 8,300-square-foot home, constructed from brick with exquisite limestone trim on the exterior, featured Arts and Crafts detailing throughout. In the 1920s, Lewis Jones decided to move his family and his 8,300-square-foot house, brick by brick, to Provencal Road. (Courtesy of HMA.)

301 Lake Shore Road. Completed in 1904, the residence at 301 Lake Shore Road is one of the oldest surviving turn-of-the-century summer cottages in the community. Carl E. Schmidt, owner of a leather tannery in Detroit, commissioned it. During the 1920s, the house was extensively remodeled to make it more suitable as a year-round home. It is listed in the National Register of Historic Places. (Courtesy of HMA.)

365 Lake Shore Road. The Victorian Queen Anne–style home was completed in 1896 as a summer cottage for John Wynne Jr., a Detroit attorney. During this era, Lake Shore Road was a premium location for wealthy Detroit businessman to build summer residences. Many of the cottages were created in a Gothic Revival or a Queen Anne style and boasted well-manicured lawns and elegant flower gardens. (Courtesy of HMA.)

1006 Bedford Road. This Colonial residence is one of a handful of homes in Grosse Pointe designed by the firm of John C. Stahl and Donald L. Kinsey. Stahl had a stellar reputation as a skilled designer of churches and schools. He also created many fine residences, including 1006 Bedford Road in 1919 for John H. Tigchon, one of Detroit's best-known and successful realtors. (Courtesy of HOD.)

71 Lake Shore Drive. The Poplars was originally a Queen Anne cottage. It was completed in 1884 for William A. McGraw, the son of A.C. McGraw, whose commercial firm was one of the most successful in Detroit. It was originally situated on a 10-acre lot that stretched from the lake to GP Boulevard. In 1927, it was enlarged and redesigned by architect Robert O. Derrick to create a Colonial-style home. (Courtesy of HOD.)

1251 Devonshire Road. John W. Case created this classically styled, wood-clad Colonial home in 1918 for George W. Yeoman, the sales and advertising manager of the Continental Motor Company. John W. Case, along with Albert Kahn and Louis Kamper, were all members of the Detroit Architectural Sketch Club, which gave public lectures on architectural history. (Courtesy of HMA.)

487 Rivard Boulevard. Bernard Stroh Jr., former president of the Stroh Brewery Company, commissioned Esselstyn and Murphy to create a large clapboard Colonial home, which was completed in 1919. This architectural style was extremely popular on Rivard Boulevard during this era, when many of the larger properties were constructed. The grand 6,299-square-foot residence is located on a huge lot that runs the entire width of St. Paul Street, from Rivard Boulevard, to University Place. (Courtesy of HMA.)

26

1011 YORKSHIRE ROAD. Ladue & Rahles completed the historic Colonial in 1916 for Edmund F. Poupard. The property, one of the earlier homes on Yorkshire Road, was part of the large Poupard Farm—one of the original ribbon farms that once lined the shores of Lake St. Clair. The home at 1011 Yorkshire Road replaced what was the original Poupard farmhouse and remained in the Poupard family until 1963. (Courtesy of HMA.)

243 LAKELAND STREET. Bernard C. Wetzel completed the grand 9,572-square-foot Tudor residence in 1915 for Daniel T. Crowley, general manager of the Peninsular Stove Work. During his career, Wetzel, a self-employed architect, was associated with some of the leading architects in the city. Aside from his residential work, he also designed a number of schools. It appears that 243 Lakeland Street was possibly his only project in the community. (Courtesy of HMA.)

1008 BISHOP ROAD. Noted Cleveland-based architects Meade and Hamilton completed 1008 Bishop Road in 1919 for Maj. James G. Heaslet, Studebaker's vice president of engineering. It is believed to be the only work in Grosse Pointe by this talented duo. During their 30-year collaboration, they reportedly designed more than 800 homes, many of which were created for the wealthy industrialists and professionals of Cleveland. (Courtesy of HMA.)

1 RATHBONE PLACE. Louis Kamper created this Italian villa–inspired residence between 1917 and 1918 for John G. Rumney, president of the Detroit Steel Products Company. Originally situated on one acre of land, the property ran from the lake to Jefferson Avenue. The garage and chauffeur's quarters were on Jefferson Avenue, with a greenhouse attached, while the stunning terraced gardens overlooked the lake. The 7,600-square-foot home is filled with superb architectural details. (Courtesy of HMA.)

Two

Masters of Architecture, the Golden Generation

During the early 20th century, the city of Detroit was home to a number of nationally recognized architects. Many of these men were responsible for creating the iconic buildings seen in Detroit today and can be credited with influencing, shaping, and changing the city's architectural landscape.

Whilst these designers created a multitude of commercial and industrial buildings, they were also responsible for producing some remarkable residences in and around Metro Detroit, including Grosse Pointe. As wealthy Detroiters began to relocate to the suburbs, they commissioned these talented artists to create grand mansions on expansive lots, many of which still exist today.

The masters of architecture are the golden generation, a group of designers who worked during a specific period of time—1900 through 1930. They can never be replaced in terms of sheer natural talent and include nationally recognized names such as Albert Kahn, Louis Kamper, George D. Mason, William Buck Stratton, and C. Howard Crane.

Between them they have designed a significant number of homes in Grosse Pointe. George D. Mason, who was once described as "the dean of Detroit architects" by renowned Detroit historian Clarence M. Burton, first appeared in Grosse Pointe around 1882 when his firm, Mason & Rice, was commissioned to design Edgmere for Joseph Berry, one of the first grand year-round homes in the community (now demolished). During his career, Mason was also responsible for training the likes of Albert Kahn, William B. Stratton, and Charles Kotting.

As their careers evolved, so too did their styles and the trends that influenced them. Throughout their careers, many of these designers elected to spend time studying architecture in England, France, and Italy, often traveling with their clients to gather inspiration. This nonstop learning curve clearly influenced their work and helped provide Grosse Pointe with the eclectic mix of homes that make the area so architecturally unique.

GEORGE D. MASON, 109 KENWOOD ROAD. George DeWitt Mason was born in 1856 in Syracuse, New York, and moved to Detroit in 1870. Having graduated in 1873, he started his career in the office of renowned architectural firm Smith, Hinchman & Grylls. By 1878, he had joined Zachariah Rice to form the firm of Mason & Rice. The partnership lasted 20 years, during which they received their first commission, in Grosse Pointe, to design one of the first year-round homes in the area—Edgemere, for Joseph Berry—located at 50 Lake Shore Drive (now demolished). In 1920, Mason organized the firm George D. Mason & Co. During his career, Mason created some of Detroit's most recognizable buildings and multiple homes in Grosse Pointe. In 1929, Lynn McNaughton, vice president of sales at Cadillac, commissioned him to design a large Tudor residence at 109 Kenwood Road in GP Farms. It was extensively damaged by fire at some point but was restored to Mason's original specifications. (Courtesy of HMA.)

GEORGE D. MASON, 33 OLDBROOK LANE. In 1920, George D. Mason designed this Tudor Revival–inspired residence for John T. Woodhouse, one of Detroit's leading tobacco merchants. The original address of East Hall was 325 Lake Shore Road. The front overlooked the lake, while the rear faced Grosse Pointe Boulevard. Beginning in the 1930s, the land was subdivided for the construction of new homes. It is listed in the National Register of Historic Places. (Courtesy of HMA.)

GEORGE D. MASON, 1040 HARVARD ROAD. This stately Colonial home was one of George D. Mason's independent projects in Grosse Pointe. Located on a multiple lot, it was completed in 1916 for John W. Staley, one of the best known of the younger bank officers in the United States. Mason played a huge part in influencing the architectural scene in Metro Detroit, particularly during the 1920s. (Courtesy of HMA.)

LOUIS KAMPER, 251 LINCOLN ROAD. Along with Albert Kahn and George D. Mason, Louis Kamper was one of the most influential architects to grace Metro Detroit. Born in 1861 in Bavaria, Germany, Kamper immigrated to the United States in 1880 with his family. In 1888, he came to Detroit. He joined the firm of Scott & Scott and made partner within a year. His list of prominent clientele grew quickly, and he received many prestigious commissions from some of Detroit's wealthiest families. During his career, Kamper continued to travel in Europe, gathering inspiration for both his commercial and residential projects. This included the Neo-Renaissance–inspired Book Cadillac Hotel, completed in 1923. At the time, it was the tallest hotel in the world. He designed multiple homes in Grosse Pointe. One of his more notable projects was 251 Lincoln Road. The Italian Renaissance–inspired home was completed in 1917 for Murray W. Sales, a manufacturer in Detroit. Louis Kamper is credited with designing over 100 commercial and residential structures in and around the city. (Courtesy of HMA.)

Louis Kamper, 15440 Windmill Pointe. In 1921, Louis Kamper designed this splendid French chateaux for Herbert V. Book, a prominent businessman and joint owner of the Book Cadillac Hotel. The cost to build the residence was reportedly around $650,000 (around $9.5 million today), with Book paying an additional $50,000 for the land (around $700,000 today). It was demolished in 1978 after being badly damaged by fire. (Courtesy of HMA.)

Louis Kamper, 175 Merriweather Road. Louis Kamper designed this Colonial–style home in 1929 as a wedding present for his niece Paula Kling and her new husband, John Robert Sutton Jr. Completed in 1931, it was one of the earliest homes to be constructed on Merriweather Road and is considerably different from Kamper's earlier projects in the community. At 3,774 square feet, it is also Kamper's smallest residential project in Grosse Pointe. (Courtesy of HMA.)

SMITH, HINCHMAN & GRYLLS (SHG), 224 VENDOME ROAD. SHG is one of the oldest architectural firms in America. Sheldon Smith, a self-taught architect, formed the practice in Ohio in 1853, having gained experience with his brother, an architect on the East Coast. In 1855, he relocated the company to Detroit. After several years, the firm had gained a stellar reputation as a place for up-and-coming architects to train, which included a young George D. Mason. The firm specialized in creating large commercial and civic structures in Metro Detroit and continued to expand. In 1896, a recently qualified engineer, Theodore H. Hinchman, joined the firm, followed by H.J. Maxwell Grylls in 1906 as partner. By the 1920s, SHG was creating many classically inspired residential and commercial projects across Metro Detroit and Grosse Pointe, including Stevens T. Mason Elementary School (1926), the new clubhouse for the Country Club of Detroit (1927), and 224 Vendome Road, Hinchman's own Tudor-inspired residence. (Courtesy of HMA.)

SMITH, HINCHMAN & GRYLLS (SHG), 35 FISHER ROAD. Completed in 1909 by SHG, this was originally the Home Telephone Company building, Grosse Pointe's first telephone office. For eight years, it was a place where customers could pay their phone bills and make long-distance calls to Detroit. The original business office is now the living room, the cashier's window is the first-floor lavatory, and the switchboard area is the dining room. (Courtesy of HMA.)

SMITH, HINCHMAN & GRYLLS (SHG), 15530 WINDMILL POINTE. Smith, Hinchman & Grylls designed this grand 14,547-square-foot Colonial Revival home in 1929 for Hal H. Smith, a partner in a leading Detroit law firm called Beaumont, Smith & Harris. Situated on a 1.9-acre lot, the magnificent 32-by-45-square-foot library features a beautiful cathedral ceiling and oak paneling. (Courtesy of HMA.)

WILLIAM B. STRATTON, 938 THREE MILE DRIVE. William B. Stratton was one of the most influential architects in Detroit during the early 20th century. He worked with some of the best designers the city had to offer and often played a big part in influencing trends. Along with Albert Kahn and several prominent designers, they spearheaded the growth of the Arts and Crafts movement Detroit, organizing the first exhibition in 1904. Stratton was born in Ithaca, New York, in 1865 and attended Cornell University. His first position in Detroit was as a draughtsman for the prestigious architectural firm of Mason & Rice in 1889. Throughout his career, he had the reputation of being an innovative designer with a "vigorous creative imagination," one who understood the latest trends. He worked alongside several talented partners and created many notable homes in GP, one of which was his own, 938 Three Mile Drive, a Spanish-inspired villa completed in 1927 for him and his wife, the noted ceramic artist Mary Chase Stratton. (Courtesy of HOD.)

WILLIAM B. STRATTON, 365 UNIVERSITY PLACE. During his career, William B. Stratton worked with a number of prominent architects. From 1918 to 1925, he was primarily associated with Dalton J. Snyder, a respected designer who lived in Grosse Pointe. Together they created several large homes in GP, including 365 University Place in 1923 for Charles B. DuCharme. (Courtesy of HMA.)

WILLIAM B. STRATTON, 7 WOODLAND PLACE. Frances Pingree, wife of the 24th governor of the state of Michigan, Hazen S. Pingree, commissioned William B. Stratton to design a summer residence. Completed in 1909, it was one of the first houses to be constructed on this once heavily wooded area. In 1935, the Dutch Colonial property received extensive alterations, by Hugh T. Keyes, to convert it from a summer home to a year-round residence. (Courtesy of HMA.)

MARCUS BURROWES, 34 BEVERLY ROAD. Marcus Burrowes was born in Tonawanda, New York, near Buffalo, in 1874. After working in Canada, he arrived in Detroit around the beginning of the 20th century. In 1905, he worked in the offices of Albert Kahn. He then joined the firm of Stratton and Baldwin, in 1907. He worked alongside many of the city's most talented designers and quickly became a respected figure. Burrowes had a stellar reputation throughout southeastern Michigan for his English Revival–style residences and also served as president of the Michigan Society of Architects. During his career, Burrowes designed more than 1,000 structures in and around the city. In 1913, Marcus Burrowes designed 34 Beverly Road, a 10,450-square-foot English Cottage residence for Sidney Trowbridge Miller, a managing partner at Michigan's oldest law firm, Miller Canfield. Burrowes designed multiple homes in Grosse Pointe, along with several other joint projects in conjunction with Frank Eurich and Dalton Wells, respectively. (Courtesy of HOD.)

Marcus Burrowes, 315 Washington Road. This Tudor and early English Renaissance mansion was designed by Marcus Burrowes for Ralph Harmon Booth, president of Booth newspapers and a major arts patron in Detroit. Completed in 1923, the 11,505-square-foot home is constructed from brick and stone and includes a fireplace and walnut paneling imported from England, along with hand-carved columns from Scotland. (Courtesy of HMA.)

Marcus Burrowes, 1018 Bishop Road. In 1920, Marcus Burrowes designed a French Normandy–style home at 1018 Bishop Road for Berrien C. Eaton, president of the Eaton Clark Company, manufacturers and importers of chemicals and dyestuffs. That same year, Burrowes joined forces with Frank Eurich (a graduate from Cornell University), and together they designed several homes in Grosse Pointe during the 1920s. (Courtesy of HOD.)

ALBERT KAHN, THE FORD ESTATE. Albert Kahn is one of the most influential architects to have graced Detroit. During his career, he designed hundreds of buildings in Metro Detroit, including commercial buildings, churches, residences, and ground-breaking industrial structures. In Grosse Pointe, he created many residences. Kahn was born in Rhaunen, Kingdom of Prussia, in 1869. His family immigrated to the United States in 1880. As a teenager he landed an apprenticeship with the prestigious firm of Mason & Rice; during this time he won a year's scholarship to study in Europe. In 1895, he and his brother Julius founded Albert Kahn Associates. Together, they developed a new type of construction method for industrial buildings that replaced many of the wooden elements (factory walls, roofs, etc.) with reinforced concrete. His residential work was also in high demand. Edsel Ford commissioned Kahn to design a picturesque Cotswold-inspired property. Construction of the 60-room house began in 1926 and took three years to complete—one year for the house and two years to custom fit the numerous antique interior elements. The Fords moved into the house in December 1929. (Courtesy of HOD.)

ALBERT KAHN, 266 LAKELAND STREET. Albert Kahn designed the elegant Tudor residence in 1912 for Benjamin F. Tobin, president of Continental Motors. Named Rosecroft because of the rose gardens that were once located on the grounds, it was one of the first properties created for the many high-profile auto executives who wanted a stunning home in the new thriving community of Grosse Pointe at the turn of the 20th century. (Courtesy of HMA.)

ALBERT KAHN, 1017 LAKE SHORE ROAD. Designed by Albert Kahn, this Cotswold-inspired cottage was completed in 1930. Set on 1.1 acres, it was originally used as the groundskeeper's house for the Ford Estate. Fifty-seven large trees, some of which still remain, once surrounded it. It appears the 2,150-square-foot brick-built residence was sold as a private home in 1948 to Theodore McGraw. (Courtesy of HMA.)

CHARLES HOWARD CRANE, 38 MCKINLEY PLACE. A prominent architect in Detroit, Crane's portfolio could be viewed as one of the more diverse of any designer in the early 20th century. During his career, he created many spectacular residences, more than 250 theaters worldwide (including at least 60 in Metro Detroit), and numerous office buildings, along with the Earls Court Exhibition Center in London. Born in 1885 in Hartford, Connecticut, Crane relocated to Detroit at the turn of the 20th century. It is believed that he worked in the offices of Albert Kahn and Smith, Hinchman & Grylls. In 1911, Crane was commissioned to design the Columbia Theater, the first movie theater in the city of Detroit. In 1915, he created the Majestic Theater; at the time it was the largest theater in the world built for the purpose of showing movies. In Grosse Pointe he designed several homes, including 38 McKinley Place, an Arts and Crafts–inspired home, along with several commercial buildings. In 1930, he moved to England, where he remained until his death in 1952. (Courtesy of HMA.)

C. Howard Crane, 69 Cloverly Road. From 1927 to 1930, C. Howard Crane designed three homes on Cloverly Road—numbers 63, 69, and 79. They covered several architectural approaches, such as Colonial, French, and Tudor. Given that the three homes were designed within three years of each other, they perfectly demonstrate Crane's diverse portfolio. No. 69 was a French-inspired home, completed in 1929 for George R. Fink, president of the National Steel Corporation. (Courtesy of HOD.)

C. Howard Crane, 1048 Yorkshire Road. C. Howard Crane completed this Regency-inspired residence in 1917 for Bertrand C. Spitzley, president of the Houseman-Spitzley Corporation and one of Detroit's best-known and successful realtors. It was one of Crane's earlier homes in the community and very different from any of his other projects in Grosse Pointe. (Courtesy of HMA.)

CHITTENDEN & KOTTING, 35 AND 43 MCKINLEY PLACE. During their 13 years working together, this talented duo created several homes in GP. Their first was 35 McKinley Place, completed in 1909, an English-style residence for David Gray, son of John Gray, the first president of the Ford Motor Company. The 7,000-square-foot, three-story house is constructed from double brick walls and finished in stucco. The garden once featured a box elder tree, several oaks, and a particularly rare ancient ginkgo tree. Six years later, in 1915, they completed another English-inspired residence, 43 McKinley Place, for Dr. Ernest T. Tappey, one of the leading physicians and surgeons of Detroit. The 8,500-square-foot, three-story residence features 16-inch concrete floors and was one of the larger, more prominent homes constructed in GP Farms during this era. (Both, courtesy of HMA.)

CHITTENDEN & KOTTING, 1014 BISHOP ROAD. In 1914, Chittenden & Kotting completed this large Colonial Revival home for Harry C. Walker, president of Walker & Co, an outdoor-advertising company. It was one of the earliest homes to be built on Bishop Road and was positioned to ensure it had maximum impact when coming up the street. During its history, it has been home to several prominent families, including Oscar Webber and Emil Stroh. (Courtesy of HOD.)

ALVIN E. HARLEY, 273 RIDGE ROAD. This superb example of a French Normandy design is one of the most distinctive homes in Grosse Pointe. Completed in 1928 for Owen R. Skelton, chief design engineer at Chrysler and member of the Automotive Hall of Fame, it is attributed to Alvin E. Harley. It is located on an unusually shaped lot; the driveway can be accessed from Ridge Road and Vendome Road. (Courtesy of HOD.)

ALVIN E. HARLEY, 895 EDGEMONT PARK AND 1005 THREE MILE DRIVE. Alvin E. Harley was a respected architect who created many grand residences in some of Detroit's more prestigious neighborhoods. Born in Canada in 1884, Harley joined Albert Kahn Associates at aged 19. He stayed with them for two years before joining the acclaimed firm of George D. Mason. From 1908 to 1912, Harley had his own practice with Norma H. Atcheson. He then set up his own firm, one that still exists today under the name of Harley Ellis Devereaux. Harley created many superb residences for Detroit's elite, including 895 Edgemont Park and 1005 Three Mile Drive in 1925 for Edward S. Evans, chairman of the Detroit Aircraft Corporation. It is a superb Tudor Revival home, located on a 50,000-square-foot parklike lot. Harley was associated with some of the best architectural talent in Detroit; he designed several homes in GPP. (Both, courtesy of HMA.)

Three

THE ROARING TWENTIES

The Roaring Twenties was a boom time for many cities in the United States. It was a time of prosperity, change, and growth. It was also a time of architectural significance and transformation, nationally and across Metro Detroit, in particular Grosse Pointe.

During the first two decades of the 20th century, Grosse Pointe had transformed itself from a rural, recreational community to an exclusive suburb in southeast Michigan. The area, up until that point, had been a haven for summer recreational cottages for wealthy Michigan families who wanted to spend their summers on the lake. The vernacular houses that were present around the area were typical of the homes found in southeast Michigan, and their architectural style was readily identifiable. However, as American prospered so did Grosse Pointe. During the 1920s, the community witnessed extensive growth and development, which ushered in a range of new architectural approaches. The styles of homes and nonresidential buildings were becoming more varied, thanks in part to the prominent architects but also to the evolving trends coming from Europe.

The large Colonial and Georgian Revival mansions were still as popular as ever, but Italian Renaissance, Mediterranean, and French influences were now becoming increasingly popular throughout Grosse Pointe during the mid- to late 1920s. French architectural style in particular had become popular in the United States shortly after World War I when French chateaus became a model of inspiration.

This period also witnessed many communities undergoing significant development, especially in Windmill Pointe and Grosse Pointe Farms. During the 1920s, Windmill Pointe was the height of popularity and became a much sought after area.

The Roaring Twenties had a profound influence on Grosse Pointe as a whole. The population of Grosse Pointe, the cities, and the architecture would never be the same again.

1004 Three Mile Drive. Local architect Hugh Taylor Millar designed this home in 1928 for Bartholomew Manning, a respected figure in the banking fraternity of Detroit. Millar created multiple homes in the community, most of which were completed during the 1920s and 1930s. Many of his designs featured dominant elements on the front elevation such as an elaborate entrance or an oversized chimney. (Courtesy of HMA.)

340 Lakeland Street. Charles Crombie and Henry F. Stanton completed this large English manor home in 1925 for Dr. Arthur B. McGraw. The 8,625-square-foot house is located on a 1.14-acre lot. As with many Crombie and Stanton projects, the exterior features beautiful intricate brickwork—in this case three magnificent interlocking brick chimneys dominate the front facade—and the entrance is wonderfully detailed. (Courtesy of HMA.)

61 Kenwood Road. The Dutch Colonial Revival home was completed in 1929 by the firm of Weston and Ellington for William Ledyard Mitchell Jr. Constructed of whitewashed brick and white clapboard, Dutch Colonial homes were becoming increasingly popular throughout Grosse Pointe during this era. The residence at 61 Kenwood Road is one of the few homes Weston and Ellington created in the community; they tended to specialize in factories and commercial buildings. (Courtesy of HMA.)

Joy Bells. The Joy Bells belonged to the Joy family and were once part of the grand Henry Joy estate, known as Fair Acres, on Lake Shore Road. In 1929, Henry B. Joy commissioned the Paccard Foundry, in the French Alps, to design and cast the bells. After the Joy estate was demolished in the late 1950s, the tower and the bells were given to the City of Grosse Pointe Farms. Having been relocated twice, they have stood in their present location since 1992. (Courtesy of HOD.)

699 Lake Shore Road. Previously known as Shadowland (due to the large number of trees on the front lawn), 699 Lake Shore Road was designed by Maul and Lentz in 1924 for Ray Danaher, a prominent lumber dealer. When the property was first built, it was situated on a three-acre lot. During the 1970s, the lot was divided into four, three lots were sold, and the house now sits on 1.25 acres. It is an excellent example of a formal Georgian property, which was particularly popular in Grosse Pointe during the 1920s. The home is constructed from brick with beautiful limestone detailing. Particularly striking are the limestone quoins on the corners of the home, along with the lintels above the front door and each of the windows. The architects, Walter Maul and Walter Lenz, both graduates of the University of Michigan, designed many homes in the affluent suburbs of Metro Detroit during the 1920s and 1930s, including several in Grosse Pointe. (Courtesy of HMA.)

78 LAKE SHORE DRIVE. Prominent local architect Hugh T. Keyes designed this French Normandy–inspired home in 1928 for Marion Dwyer Palms and Charles Palms. When the house was completed, it was the first one in the area to be wired for a telephone; it housed a circuit board in the garage for the neighborhood phones. The interior had 150-year-old fireplace mantels, a sweeping staircase, curved hallways, and an unusual circular floor plan. (Courtesy of HMA.)

456 UNIVERSITY PLACE. Prior to 1914, Charles Lewis Phelps had worked for George Mason, John Scott & Co., and Albert Kahn Associates. He designed this Mediterranean Revival–style home in 1925 for Gertrude Baker. The Mediterranean style was popular throughout the United States, peaking in popularity during the 1920s and 1930s. There are several superb examples of Mediterranean-inspired homes throughout Grosse Pointe. (Courtesy of HMA.)

Grosse Pointe High School. The school has come a long way since the property, 23 acres of swampland, was purchased from Helen Newberry and the McMillan family. Completed in 1928, it was designed by local architect George J. Hass. The Neo-Georgian–inspired building features a dominant 134-foot-tall clock tower. At the time of completion, the clock tower was the highest architectural structure in the Pointes. The first class to grace the building was in 1928. During the 1930s, the number of students enrolled at the school was 1,340, just short of the maximum capacity. To make more room, the board of education offices were relocated to the Cadieux Elementary School, on St. Clair Avenue, where they remain today. Since then, the building has continued to evolve. Despite the expansion over the years, the integrity of the original design has remained, and the school has become everything it was intended to be—one of the best public schools in the state of Michigan. (Courtesy of HOD.)

257 Ridge Road. Completed in 1929, this Tudor–inspired residence was designed by Albert Kahn for the successful sheet music publisher Jerome H. Remick. The 9,346-square-foot residence, constructed from limestone and brick, includes an attached four-car heated garage with a chauffeur's apartment above. The living room is said to closely resemble the living room in the Edsel Ford House, which Kahn also completed in 1929. (Courtesy of HMA.)

21 Colonial Road. Local architect Robert F. Swanson designed this Mediterranean-inspired home in 1928 for Carrado Parducci, a nationally recognized sculptor known for his mid-20th-century works. Parducci was one of the most respected sculptors of the early 20th century. He worked on many significant buildings in Detroit and with some of the leading architects in the city. (Courtesy of HMA.)

A Sears Catalog Home, 849 Notre Dame Street. One of the finest examples in Grosse Pointe of a 1920s kit home is 849 Notre Dame Street. Built in 1926, this was a Sears Catalog Home (sold under the name of Sears Modern Homes), which were sold across the United States between 1908 and 1940. The catalog presented 370 different models in various architectural styles. The house at 849 Notre Dame Street was constructed from a kit called the "Kilbourne." The Craftsman-inspired design was a 1,450-square-foot, five-room bungalow. It came already cut and fitted but did not include the cement, brick, or plaster. The owners then hired a contractor to build their home. It is believed that around 70,000 Modern Homes were sold by Sears; the majority are located on the East Coast and in the Midwest. It appears that this is the only authenticated Sears Modern Home in Grosse Pointe. (Courtesy of HMA.)

CRAFTSMAN HOMES, 844 BARRINGTON ROAD. Toward the latter end of the Arts and Crafts movement came Craftsman homes. Dominant characteristics include a large front porch, low-pitched gabled roof, and deep overhanging eaves. One of the best examples of a Craftsman bungalow in the community is 844 Barrington Road, built in 1927. (Courtesy of HMA.)

THE STERLING KIT HOME, 1100 BISHOP ROAD. Sterling Homes was a leading manufacturer of kit homes. One of the few authenticated models in Grosse Pointe is 1100 Bishop Road, purchased and completed in 1921 by contractor Alexander Russell Keys for his family. It is constructed from a kit called the "Vernon." The Colonial-inspired design was one of the larger kit homes on the market during this era. (Courtesy of HOD.)

THE FORD ESTATE, THE GATE LODGE. Located at Gaulker Pointe, Grosse Pointe Shores, the Ford Estate was completed in 1929 for Edsel and Eleanor Ford. Designed by Albert Kahn, it was set on a 125-acre estate. It took nearly 14 years to complete the residence, beginning in 1926 and culminating in 1940. The Fords hired some of the best designers around. Aside from Albert Kahn, who designed the house, estate perimeter wall, gate lodge, north and south cottages,

and the recreation building, the Fords hired Danish-born designer Jens Jensen, one of the 20th century's most influential landscape architects. His time at the Ford Estate resulted in the creation of one of the most beautiful gardens in southeastern Michigan. Today, the estate is around 87 acres. (Photograph by Thomas Ellison; courtesy of the Edsel and Eleanor Ford House.)

EDSEL AND ELEANOR FORD'S BEDROOM, 1935; AND ELEANOR FORD STANDING IN FRONT OF A RENOIR PAINTING, 1960. The interior of the Ford Estate was incredibly detailed. The majority of the finishes and architectural elements were chosen to compliment the Tudor Revival style. Many of the rooms on the main floor feature carved paneling, stone and wood mantels, and decorative plaster, some of which were imported from manor houses in England. Despite the formal approach to much of the interior, the bedrooms for the Ford's three sons and their connected sitting rooms were redecorated in the 1930s by Walter Dorwin Teague, an industrial designer, with a superb Art Deco approach. The residence has 60 rooms, including the servants' quarters. (Both, courtesy of the Edsel and Eleanor Ford House.)

329 GROSSE POINTE BOULEVARD. The Detroit firm of Esselstyn, Murphy & Burns created this Mediterranean-inspired home in 1922. It has superb architectural features, including an abundance of arches on the entranceway and above the first-floor windows. Between 1924 through 1929, designer Horace H. Esselstyn partnered with prominent local architect Raymond Carey to create several prestigious homes in Grosse Pointe. (Courtesy of HMA.)

379 LAKELAND STREET. Hugh T. Keyes completed this Tudor Revival–style house in 1926 for investment banker Jerome E. Keane and his wife, Annette Dwyer. The house is located on part of the original Dwyer estate (owned by Annette's parents), as was the property's large formal garden. Keyes surrounded the property with a large wall, which he incorporated into the brick facade of the house. (Courtesy of HMA.)

745 BALFOUR STREET. This home was a collaborative project in 1925 between Detroit architects J. Ivan Dise and Clair William Ditchy for Harry J. Stoops, vice president and general manager of the American Cycle Car Co. However, noted local architect Leonard B. Willeke completed it in 1927. Willeke also designed the garage, greenhouse, and the gardens at the residence. The Colonial-style home, located on three lots, features a utility elevator that ran from the basement to the second floor and a separate two-story carriage house with a basement that was connected to the main residence by the greenhouse. The large 38-foot-by-18-foot heated greenhouse contained a deep storage pond located under one of the planting beds. During the winter, it was filled with koi that were moved indoors from the outside pond. In 1941, 745 Balfour Street became one of the first homes in Grosse Pointe to be fully air-conditioned when two 3.5-ton air-conditioning units were installed. They had to be located in a room of their own. (Courtesy of HMA.)

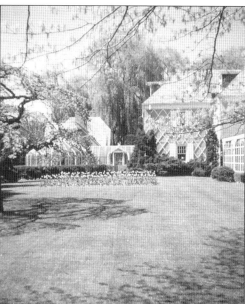

745 BALFOUR STREET GARDENS. Architect Leonard B. Willeke was also an accomplished landscape designer. The garden he created at 745 Balfour Street was beautiful, filled with mature elms, fruit trees, a sea of tulips, and a two-story high lattice on the back fence that was covered with morning glories. It also contained a large pond filled with koi and a sunken rock garden. (Both, courtesy of William Doelle.)

930 LAKE SHORE ROAD. Beckett and Akitt designed this English-style manor for Clarence Ayers. It was completed in 1928. Beckitt and Akitt worked together in Detroit from 1920 until 1934, specialized in designing large residences in Michigan and Metro Detroit. Between 1926 and 1931, they completed several homes in Grosse Pointe in a variety of architectural styles. (Courtesy of HMA.)

2 WOODLAND PLACE. Despite specializing in Georgian-inspired residences, Robert O. Derrick was an incredibly versatile designer. He completed this Federal-style residence in 1928 for Florence Eddy. Her husband, Frank Woodman Eddy, was a prominent businessman in Detroit who had made his fortune from chemical and rubber manufacturing. In 1940, Emory Moran Ford purchased the home and hired Hugh T. Keyes to make extensive alterations. (Courtesy of HMA.)

4 WOODLAND PLACE. William B. Stratton and Dalton J. Snyder created this 5,450-square-foot Colonial home in 1920 for John R. Russel, the secretary and treasurer of the Russel Wheel and Foundry Company. The home at 4 Woodland Place was Stratton's second project on the street, having completed 7 Woodland Place in 1911. He and Dalton Snyder worked together from 1915 to 1925 and completed several homes in the community. (Courtesy of HMA.)

15500 WINDMILL POINTE. This Tudor Revival–inspired residence was created in 1930 by Benjamin and Straight for Col. Jesse G. Vincent, American aircraft designer and head of engineering at the Packard Motor Car Company. The 5,256-square-foot residence is particularly unique in that the canal, in the back garden, runs from Lake. St. Clair to a large door at the rear of the home, which opens up to reveal a dry dock that is located in the basement, underneath the living room. Other special features contained in this home are a large 47-by-19-square-foot ballroom on the third floor and a semicircular-shaped sitting room on the second floor with a conical-shaped roof. The living room has a distinctive stone fireplace and a partially paneled balcony, the kitchen contains a six-door oak-paneled refrigerator, and the basement includes a tavern room and access to the heated greenhouse in the garden. (Courtesy of HMA.)

15410 Windmill Pointe. This English-inspired manor house was designed by Alfred Hopkins & Associates and completed in 1924 for William P. Harris, an investment banker and father of stage actress Julie Harris. The stonework features many beautiful carvings of clipper ships and gargoyles. In 1929, the size of the house increased dramatically after Harris hired noted architect Hugh T. Keyes to expand it. (Courtesy of HMA.)

15420 Windmill Pointe. Robert O. Derrick designed Bellmor in 1927 for John B. Moran, whose family were huge landowners in the community. It is believed that the home is modeled on an historic English manor house, Compton Wynyates, that Moran was said to be a fan of after a trip to England in the early 1920s. It is alleged that the house narrowly avoided demolition in the 1970s. (Courtesy of HMA.)

15520 WINDMILL POINTE. This Georgian Revival mansion designed by Alpheus Chittenden was completed in 1903 for John B. Ford. Its original location was in Indian Village; however, in 1928, it was moved by truck under the supervision of leading architect Charles Kotting to its new location on Windmill Pointe by John B. Ford's son and daughter-in-law, Frederick and Esther Ford. (Courtesy of HMA.)

15366 WINDMILL POINTE. Renowned architect William B. Stratton completed this distinguished 13,000-square-foot Tudor home in 1928 for Julian H. Harris, a prominent lawyer in the city of Detroit. The design combines traditional details associated with the Tudor architectural approach with fine craftsmanship and independent touches that were unique to Stratton. Nationally recognized landscape architect Ellen Shipman designed the garden. (Courtesy of HMA.)

30 PRESTON PLACE. During the early 1920s, Louise Webber, niece of J.L. Hudson, commissioned renowned New York architect Duncan Candler to design a summer residence in GP Farms. The house was finally completed around 1932. The delay was due, in part, to the unexpected death of Louise Webber's husband, Roscoe Jackson, in 1929, along with the Great Depression. Set on 10 acres of land, the original address of the 9,000-square-foot house was 486 Kercheval Avenue. In 1961, Edward P. Frohlich purchased the estate. It soon became the location for many lavish parties and social gatherings. Over time, the family subdivided the estate to create the Preston Place subdivision. Upon his death, Frohlich requested that 30 Preston Place be left to the Detroit Symphony Orchestra (DSO) Hall Foundation. It was intended that the house would provide the president of the DSO with a permanent residence or visiting artists with a temporary base. It was listed for sale by the trust in 2016. (Courtesy of HMA.)

355 LAKELAND STREET. Charles Crombie and Henry F. Stanton completed this exquisite brick home in 1927. The French Provincial Revival–style home was allegedly built for Henry Monroe Campbell Jr. When the house was first built, the entrance featured an oversized stained-glass window depicting the Griffon, a double-mast ship, which carried the first explorers to Lake St. Clair. Crombie and Stanton designed several homes in GP. (Courtesy of HOD.)

160 TOURAINE ROAD. Carl L. Meek designed this French Colonial residence in 1928 for William Scripps, publisher of the *Detroit News* and an avid aviator. At 5,389 square feet, it was Meek's largest project in Grosse Pointe. He designed and/or built multiple homes in the community, most of which were completed during the 1920s and covered a broad spectrum of architectural styles. (Courtesy of HMA.)

225 TOURAINE ROAD. Oscar Gottesleben and Walter Bernardi completed this 4,214-square-foot home in 1927 for Ernest Bartholomaei, secretary and treasurer of building contractors Max Bartholomaei. The house remained in the family through four generations and was listed for sale in 2012 for the first time. Gottesleben was a respected architect in Detroit during the early 20th century and was an advocate of the Arts and Crafts movement. (Courtesy of HOD.)

217 TOURAINE ROAD. This grand Georgian Revival residence was completed in 1929 by August Geiger for John B. Ford. At the time, Geiger was a prestigious architect in southeastern Florida. He tended to specialize in Mediterranean-style homes but was also known to create more formal residences. This home is believed to be Geiger's sole project in the state of Michigan. In 1941, auto designer Harley Earl purchased the residence. (Courtesy of HMA.)

1007 Bishop Road. The 8,000-square-foot Tudor mansion is set on 1.5 acres. Completed in 1921, it was designed by University of Michigan graduates Walter Maul and Walter Lentz for Michael J. Murphy, president of the Murphy Chair Company in Detroit. The three-story residence features a black marble foyer with an elevator, installed when the house was built to help his wife, Elisa, reach the second floor. (Courtesy of HMA.)

1011 Bishop Road. J.H. Gustav Steffens completed this Mediterranean-inspired home in 1928 for John A. Kengel, longtime owner of a popular hardware store. Steffens was an established architect in Detroit, creating large residences in the affluent suburbs of Metro Detroit. Here in Grosse Pointe, he designed multiple homes during the 1920s and 1930s. (Courtesy of HMA.)

BLOODGOOD TUTTLE, 840 AND 920 BALFOUR STREET. Bloodgood Tuttle was a nationally recognized architect. Born in Cleveland in 1889, he graduated from the University of Chicago and also studied at the École Nationale Supérieure des Beaux-Arts in Paris. He worked primarily on residential projects and in multiple locations, creating at least 36 homes in Shaker Heights, Ohio, along with several projects throughout Michigan. He created at least three homes in Grosse Pointe. His first project here was in 1918. Smith, Hinchman & Grylls were commissioned by John Francis Dodge to create what was intended to be the largest residence in the Detroit area. It is believed that the project was assigned to Bloodgood Tuttle to design the magnificent home—223 Lake Shore Road. It was started but never completed. Tuttle then designed two striking homes on Balfour Street in 1923 for builder Herbert K. Barber. (Both, courtesy of HMA.)

175 Ridge Road. In 1920, respected designers Marcus Burrowes and Frank Eurich created the firm Burrowes and Eurich. Together, they designed several homes in Grosse Pointe, including 175 Ridge Road, a stately Georgian Colonial home, in 1922 for William H. Muir, cofounder of the Jenks & Muir Manufacturing Company and a banker. The property had a beautiful formal garden that was restored to its formal glory in 2019. (Courtesy of HMA.)

180 Ridge Road. Robert O. Derrick completed this Colonial residence in 1925 for William Ledyard Mitchell, general manager of Chrysler. The 6,208-square-foot home was constructed from wood with a wooden shingle roof. The project marked a significant departure from Derrick's formal Georgian brick houses. The garden was designed by leading New York landscape architect Ruth Bramley Dean, her third project in the community. (Courtesy of HMA.)

812 WHITTIER ROAD. George V. Pottle designed the English-style residence for Charles L. Gollarno in 1927. It appears this was Pottle's only project in Grosse Pointe. Pottle relocated to Detroit from Dayton in 1901. During his career, he worked on early cinema theater projects and numerous large industrial buildings in Detroit and designed fine residences for affluent families in the suburbs. (Courtesy of HMA.)

1305 WHITTIER ROAD. Rupert W. Koch completed this Tudor-inspired home in 1927 for James E. Sheridan. It is a unique design and is very different from most Tudor homes in the community. Koch graduated from the University of Michigan and spent most of his career in Ann Arbor. He designed several homes in Grosse Pointe, six of them during the 1920s. (Courtesy of HMA.)

1051 BERKSHIRE ROAD. Known as the "Coin de France," this French Normandy–style home was completed in 1929 for Victor R. Heftler, an engineer and president of the Zenith Carburetor Company. It is one of the few residences designed by the Detroit-based firm of Donaldson & Meier, which was well regarded in Detroit and southeastern Michigan for designing churches. (Courtesy of HOD.)

1233 KENSINGTON AVENUE. Richard E. Raseman designed this central entrance Colonial home in 1924 for Frederick J. Holtz. Raseman became a recognized architect in Detroit in 1883. He tended to specialize in industrial brewery projects and was noted for his use of heavy stone and the Richardson Romanesque architectural approach. During his long and distinguished career, he created several homes in the community. (Courtesy of HMA.)

355 Lincoln Road. The noted New York firm of Alfred Hopkins & Associates completed this 8,733-square-foot English manor in 1923 for Dr. Theodore McGraw Jr., a well-known physician in Detroit. It is one of the largest homes in Grosse Pointe City, filled with beautiful architectural details, including an 18-foot-high barrel-shaped ceiling and decorative carved limestone. Nationally renowned landscape architect Ellen Biddle Shipman designed the garden. (Courtesy of HMA.)

17315 East Jefferson Avenue. In 1927, Charles A. Platt designed this large Georgian mansion and the gardens for Grace McGraw. It is constructed from Flemish brick with a slate roof and features magnificent detailing, including a limestone sundial set into the chimney. Platt was a renowned architect, artist, and designer; he designed five grand homes in Grosse Pointe; however, only three still exist. (Courtesy of HMA.)

Four

THE PRESTIGIOUS ARCHITECTS OF THE 1920S AND 1930S

The 1920s and 1930s were a time of architectural transformation in Grosse Pointe. While the architectural masters were still creating grand homes, they were, by now, being joined by a group of talented young architects, many of whom were former protégées, who would take the architectural scene to the next level.

This core group of artists was instrumental in designing the residential, commercial, and public buildings that were created in and around Metro Detroit during this era. While most had their favored styles, they were also aware of the changing trends around them and were not afraid to add their own interpretation.

Some of the most prominent names were Hugh T. Keyes, Wallace Frost, Robert O. Derrick, J. Ivan Dise, and Leonard B. Willeke. Between them, they created multiple residences across the Grosse Pointe communities in numerous architectural approaches—Tudor, Georgian, Regency, French, and Colonial.

The influence these architects had on the architectural style of homes and buildings in Grosse Pointe, particularly in GP Farms was astonishing. Their designs were integral in transforming the style of homes that were built throughout the community during this era. Not only did this lead to developing a consistent look and feel, but also arguably influenced the work of lesser-known architects who were hired to create smaller homes.

As these artists headed into the 1930s, their work was influenced by numerous factors—the Great Depression, the desire for smaller homes, the economic and geographical changes to the community, and the ever-evolving design trends from both national and international sources.

Hugh T. Keyes, for instance, stayed ahead of the curve. During the 1930s, his style started to migrate away from the traditional forms to what would become his post-1930 distinctive white brick Regency approach. Many of these men were also hired to transform some of the existing larger mansions into more livable spaces for modern living.

Welcome to the dawn of a new age!

HUGH T. KEYES, 344 PROVENCAL ROAD. One of the most prolific architects in Metro Detroit was Hugh Tallman Keyes. His work spanned several decades and crossed many significant periods of architectural styles. Born in 1888 in Trenton, Michigan, Hughes studied architecture at Harvard University. He landed his first significant job in the studio of respected designer C. Howard Crane and was also an associate of Albert Kahn. During World War I, Keyes spent two years serving in the Navy, after which he travelled extensively in Europe, which heavily influenced his architectural career. By 1921, Keyes had formed his own practice. He was an incredibly versatile designer; his style ranged from Tudor Revival and Georgian to his Regency Moderne approach. He received many prestigious commissions, including several grand estates for the industrialists of Metro Detroit. He designed multiple homes in Grosse Pointe, including 344 Provencal Road, completed in 1929 for Henry P. Williams. The majority of his commissions in the community were between the 1920s and early 1950s, including making extensive additions to older mansions for modern living. (Courtesy of HMA.)

HUGH T. KEYES, 221 LEWISTON ROAD. Hugh T. Keyes completed this Italian Renaissance–inspired villa in 1924 for Charles A. Dean. The 8,800-square-foot home, named Ridgeland, is constructed of tawny bricks with a red tile roof. It is located on a sloping ridge surrounded by large oak trees, thereby evoking a country house flowing down a hillside in Tuscany. (Courtesy of HMA.)

HUGH T. KEYES, 22 LEE GATE LANE. Hugh T. Keyes built many notable houses during his career. One of his principal works was 22 Lee Gate Lane, completed in 1947 for Robert Hudson Tannahill, a respected art collector in Detroit and nephew of Eleanor Ford. At this stage of his career, Keyes had begun to focus on what was quickly becoming his signature white brick Regency style. (Courtesy of HMA.)

CLARENCE E. DAY, 906 THREE MILE DRIVE. In 1936, Clarence E. Day adopted a Regency-style approach for this 5,800-square-foot home. This type of architecture was extremely popular during the 1930s, thanks in part to the Regency-style homes designed by Hugh T. Keyes during this period. Classic traits of this style are a symmetrical facade, hipped roof, and flat rectangular chimneys. (Courtesy of HMA.)

CLARENCE E. DAY, 1018 THREE MILE DRIVE. Clarence E. Day completed this 7,008-square-foot Tudor Revival home in 1929 for W.D. McClintock. Day's work was highly sought after during the 1920s. Between 1920 and 1940, he created several homes in the community that spanned a range of architectural styles. 1018 Three Mile Drive is a recipient of the Grosse Pointe Historical Society's bronze plaque award. (Courtesy of HMA.)

FRANK A. MILES, 60 CAMBRIDGE ROAD. Frank Miles designed multiple homes in the community between 1925 and 1950, covering a broad range of architectural styles. This home at 60 Cambridge Road was completed in 1926. The Spanish Revival–inspired residence was created during an era when Mediterranean architecture was becoming increasingly popular in Grosse Pointe. (Courtesy of HMA.)

FRANK A. MILES, 76 LOTHROP ROAD. This classic stately English-inspired residence (formerly 20 Lothrop Road) was one of Frank A. Miles's more significant projects. It was completed in 1937 for George O. Johnston. Joseph Mullen, an interior designer who was president of the American Institute of Decorators during the 1940s, decorated the interior. (Courtesy of HOD.)

ROBERT O. DERRICK, 211 VENDOME ROAD. Robert O. Derrick played a pivotal role in helping to transform the architectural scene in Grosse Pointe during the 1920s. He was a prolific architect in the community, specializing in creating large formal residences for prominent clientele who were looking for "something spectacular." Born in Buffalo, New York, Derrick graduated from Columbia University in 1917. Much of his work in Grosse Pointe occurred during the 1920s. One of his earliest projects was the Grosse Pointe Club in 1923. He then went on to design multiple homes and several public buildings, including the Grosse Pointe Farms water filtration and pumping station in 1930. In 1927, he went to England to study British Domestic Architecture. The trip fueled his love for Georgian architecture, which is evident in many of his later projects, including 211 Vendome Road, completed in 1929 for F. Caldwell Walker, grandson of whiskey baron Hiram Walker. Derrick lived with his family at 407 Lincoln Road and was a well-known figure in the community. (Courtesy of HMA.)

ROBERT O. DERRICK, 294 LINCOLN ROAD. In 1924, Robert O. Derrick completed this formal residence for Frederick W. Hodges, an industrialist and general manager of the Detroit Steam Radiator Company. This was one of Derrick's earlier projects in Grosse Pointe and was in keeping with the architectural style he favored during the early 1920s, which included 23 and 27 Beverly Road. (Courtesy of HMA.)

ROBERT O. DERRICK, 187 IRVINE LANE. Sidney T. Miller Jr., a prominent attorney in Detroit, commissioned Robert O. Derrick to design this modern yet traditional home that incorporated several Georgian-inspired details that were Derrick's signature elements. Completed in 1949, it was one of Derrick's latter projects in Grosse Pointe and very different from his earlier, much more formal houses. Noted local landscape architect Eleanor Roche designed the garden. (Courtesy of HMA.)

CHARLES KOTTING, 805 THREE MILE DRIVE AND 281 UNIVERSITY PLACE. Charles Kotting was a respected designer, creating over 100 structures, commercial and residential, in and around Metro Detroit. Born in 1865 in Holland, he graduated from school in Amsterdam and immigrated to Detroit in 1889. He joined the firm of Mason & Rice, where he would stay for 13 years. In 1903, he and Alphus Chittenden came together to create their own firm. During their 13 years together, they completed many prominent projects in Detroit and several prestigious homes in Grosse Pointe. Post 1916, now working alone, Kotting created a classically designed Tudor home in 1917 at 805 Three Mile Drive as well as 281 University Place in 1918, a grand manor home for lawyer Harold Palmer. During his career, Kotting also served as president of the Michigan Chapter of the American Institute of Architects. (Both, courtesy of HMA.)

RICHARD H. MARR, 1108 WHITTIER ROAD. Richard H. Marr was a respected residential designer in Metro Detroit during the 1920s. He created many superb homes for some of Detroit's wealthiest families and became known as the "Architect of Midwest Millionaires." Marr created around 14 homes in Palmer Woods and several properties in Grosse Pointe during the 1920s and 1930s, including the English Terrace townhouses at Rivard Boulevard and Jefferson Avenue, built between 1926 and 1929. Marr was born in Detroit in 1886. He earned a degree in architecture from Harvard University in 1911 and remained in Boston for another two years. On his return to Detroit, he primarily focused on residential projects and apartments in Detroit and the surrounding suburbs. Throughout his career, much of Marr's work was heavily influenced by the Tudor Revival style. One of his earliest projects in Grosse Pointe was 905 Balfour Street, built in 1923. In 1935, he completed the Tudor-styled 1108 Whittier Road for William F. Demske. Richard Marr was also a director for the Michigan Society of Architects. (Courtesy of HMA.)

LEONARD B. WILLEKE, 1100 BERKSHIRE ROAD. Leonard B. Willeke was a skilled and adaptable designer. He was equally capable of creating a piece of furniture or a light fixture as he was at designing a house or a garden. Willeke was a familiar face in Grosse Pointe; he and his wife resided in the community for over 50 years. Born in Cincinnati in 1889, his career began at a local architectural firm. In 1905, he moved to New York to study at Columbia University and to work for Trowbridge & Livingston. After a brief period working on a West Coast–based project, he decided to study architecture abroad at the famed École Nationale Supérieure des Beaux-Arts in Paris and tour Europe. He returned to Cincinnati with 8,000 postcards, 27 bound albums of photographs, and numerous sketchbooks. By 1916, Willeke was an established architect in Detroit with his own practice and many prestigious clients. In 1922, he designed his own home, 1100 Berkshire Road in GP Park, a striking English-inspired residence. During his career, he created multiple residences and several gardens in Grosse Pointe. (Courtesy of HMA.)

Leonard B. Willeke, 1012 Three Mile Drive. In 1929, Leonard B. Willeke designed 1012 Three Mile Drive, a Tudor-style residence for Raymond J. Purdy, chief engineer of the Ainsworth Manufacturing Company. During the 1920s, Willeke was particularly sought after. He received a number of commissions in GP Park from prominent clientele, including William A. Petzold, the vice president of J.L. Hudson and Company, who commissioned Willeke to design a large Tudor residence at 1010 Three Mile Drive in 1928. (Courtesy of HMA.)

Leonard B. Willeke, 938 Balfour Street. Leonard B. Willeke designed and built this residence in 1922 as a speculative home—"a residence built without a particular buyer in mind or under contract, but designed to appeal to the maximum market possible." It was his first of four such homes on Balfour Street constructed between 1922 and 1928. Col. Jesse Vincent, chief engineer at Packard Motor Car Company, purchased the house. (Courtesy of HMA.)

D. ALLEN WRIGHT, 79 KENWOOD ROAD. D. Allen Wright was a versatile designer who created multiple houses in Grosse Pointe. Having served in World War I, he rejoined the prominent Detroit firm of Alvin E. Harley. During the 1920s, Wright started his own practice. At this stage of his career, he predominantly focused on French-inspired architecture, in particular Normandy and Provincial styles that were popular throughout Grosse Pointe from the 1920s to the 1940s. In the span of seven years, Wright created around nine French-inspired residences in the community. This included 79 Kenwood Road, completed in 1926 for Alvan Macauley Jr., banking commissioner of Michigan and vice president of the National Bank of Detroit. During the 1930s, Wright's style evolved considerably, focusing more on trends of the Art Moderne–inspired period. In 1943, Wright was involved in a project to create an innovative postwar suburban home complete with a semicircular kitchen and curved walls. (Courtesy of HMA.)

D. ALLEN WRIGHT, 93 CLOVERLY ROAD. D. Allen Wright completed this French Normandy home in 1927 for Clarkson C. Wormer Jr., a real estate developer. Typical traits of this approach include a round stone tower topped by a conical-shaped roof, stone facade, and a steeply pitched roof. There are several superb examples of this style around the Grosse Pointe communities, with most of them built during the 1920s. (Courtesy of HMA.)

D. ALLEN WRIGHT, 166 RIDGE ROAD. Designed by D. Allen Wright, this French Normandy–inspired home was completed in 1927 for Charles F. Lambert, president of the Clayton & Lambert Manufacturing Company. French-inspired architecture was particularly popular in Grosse Pointe during the 1920s, having become fashionable in the United States shortly after World War I. (Courtesy of HMA.)

RAYMOND CAREY, 270 VOLTAIRE PLACE. Architect Raymond Carey was a prominent designer in Grosse Pointe Farms. He was born in England in 1883 and grew up in Bath, where some of the finest examples of Georgian architecture in the country can be found. He immigrated to Detroit at the beginning of the 20th century. Having spent several years working in Canada, he returned to Detroit in the 1920s, whereupon he designed numerous Georgian-inspired mansions. 270 Voltaire Place is a Georgian-inspired home built in 1929 for Sarah Macauley, wife of millinery dealer/wholesaler Richard H. Macauley; it was, at the time, one of the finest estates in Grosse Pointe. The front elevation features many beautiful carved elements, while the interior was equally as detailed. In 1929, the house cost $16,099.25 to build (around $2.4 million today). (Courtesy of HMA.)

RAYMOND CAREY, 234 PROVENCAL ROAD. Raymond Carey completed the large English Country–inspired residence in 1929 for George M. Holley, an automotive engineer and designer who cofounded the Holley Carburetor Company, the world's largest independent manufacturer of carburetors. Carey was a master at the Tudor Revival approach, which is clearly evident in his design for the 8,122-square-foot home. The residence at 234 Provencal Road is reminiscent of an English country estate. (Courtesy of HMA.)

RAYMOND CAREY, 73 MORAN ROAD. While Raymond Carey created many fine Georgian and Tudor residences for most of his clients, he created a more modest home for Walter B. Ford. Completed in 1925, it is close in style to many homes found in England during this era. It appears Carey returned to London in the late 1930s. In 1938, he was elected as a fellow of the Royal Institute of British Architects. (Courtesy of HMA.)

WALLACE FROST, 242 LEWISTON ROAD. Wallace Frost was a prolific designer in Metro Detroit. He created over 40 homes in and around Birmingham and several significant homes in Grosse Pointe. Frost was born in Union, Pennsylvania, in 1892 and studied at the University of Pennsylvania. During World War I, Frost was stationed in Washington, DC, designing hangars for military installations. During this time, he met Albert Kahn, who had great admiration for Frost's work. After the war, Frost joined Kahn in Michigan, and together they collaborated on some of Kahn's most prominent projects. In 1926, Frost started his own firm. His style during this era centered on midsize cottage houses with French and English architectural influences. During the 1930s, he spent time traveling in Europe and California. He returned to Michigan in 1931, where he continued to practice until 1961. In 1926, Frost completed 242 Lewiston Road. The French country–style residence was designed to complement the significant slope it is situated on—a "rolling country-style terrain landscaped for privacy." (Courtesy of HMA.)

WALLACE FROST, 16632 EAST JEFFERSON AVENUE. The Wallace Frost homes around Michigan are often described as "prized finds." Completed in 1926, the 6,683-square-foot French Normandy–inspired manor was designed for Edgar Bowen, vice president and secretary of the Ferry-Morse Seed Company. Frost created a number of French-inspired properties during the 1920s; however, by the early 1940s, his style was far more contemporary. (Courtesy of HMA.)

WALLACE FROST, 15324 WINDMILL POINTE. One of the more significant properties built at Windmill Pointe is Kasteel Batavia. Completed in 1927, the French Provincial–inspired home was designed by noted architect Wallace Frost for Ross W. Judson, founder of the Continental Motor Company. The residence is believed to be located on the site of a historic windmill and has one of the few remaining French missionary pear trees. (Courtesy of HMA.)

J. Ivan Dise, 130 Kenwood Road. J. Ivan Dise was a prominent and respected architect who created multiple homes in Grosse Pointe. The majority of his commissions came in the 1920s and 1930s at a time when large homes were commonplace for wealthy clientele. Dise was born in Pennsylvania in 1887. After graduating from the University of Pennsylvania in 1909, he moved to New York to begin his career with the prestigious firm of Cass Gilbert. During his time there, he worked on several projects in the city of Detroit, including the Detroit Public Library and the Scott Memorial Fountain on Belle Isle. In 1919, Dise moved to Detroit to join Albert Kahn Associates, where he would remain for three years. In 1922, he set up his own firm. During this time, he also collaborated on a number of projects in Grosse Pointe with Clair William Ditchy. In 1926, he completed 130 Kenwood Road for Luther D. Thomas. The grand 7,256-square-foot Tudor-style home was one of Dise's larger projects in the community. (Courtesy of HOD.)

J. Ivan Dise, 849 Balfour Street. This large Tudor Revival home was completed by J. Ivan Dise in 1923 for Bertrand C. Spitzley, president of the Houseman-Spitzley Corporation and one of Detroit's best-known and most successful real estate brokers and developers. Dise created numerous homes across Grosse Pointe, with multiple residences on Balfour Street, Cloverly Road, and Kenwood Road. He also designed the pumping station, located at Chalfonte Avenue and Kerby Road, in 1929. (Courtesy of HMA.)

J. Ivan Dise, 90 Kenwood Road. J. Ivan Dise completed the English-inspired home in 1929 for Cleveland Thurber, a prominent legal, business, and civic leader in Detroit. Thurber was a key member of the law firm of Miller, Canfield, Paddock & Stone from 1922 until 1980. This residence at 90 Kenwood Road is one of three homes Dise created on Kenwood between 1926 and 1929. (Courtesy of HOD.)

Omer C. Bouschor, 946 Balfour Street and 15637 Windmill Pointe. Omer C. Bouschor, a Detroit-based architect, created multiple homes in the community. During the 1930s, Bouschor designed multiple Tudor-inspired homes in Grosse Pointe. One of his earliest projects appears to be 946 Balfour Street. The 4,850-square-foot residence features a distinctive timbered and stucco section on the second floor, a classic trait of this in architectural approach. As Bouschor's career developed, so did his style. Between 1935 and 1954, he began to focus on creating more formal-style homes, along with a number of modern Colonial residences. This included 15637 Windmill Pointe, a large Southern-inspired Colonial home built in 1940 for Dr. Elden C. Baumgarten, an anesthesiologist. Between 1935 and 1948, Bouschor designed at least six large homes on Windmill Pointe. (Both, courtesy of HMA.)

Five

THE CHANGING FACE OF GROSSE POINTE

During the 1930s, Grosse Pointe began to see some significant changes—demographically, geographically, and architecturally. The traditional Georgian and Tudor homes began to receive some significantly different architectural neighbors, ones with international style.

The International style and Art Deco movement began to gather pace in the United States at the beginning of the 1930s. The city of Detroit, in particular, was a key hub for this new approach and boasts some of the finest examples of Art Deco buildings in the country.

In Grosse Pointe, leading designers who favored the Art Deco and International approach had begun to create numerous buildings in the community. Those designers included Alden Dow, Eliel Saarinen, Louis Rossetti, Lyle Zisler, and Alexander Girrard. This new approach added a different dimension to the type of residences that were being constructed in the area. They were innovative, on trend, and in a style that had never been seen in Grosse Pointe.

As these new neighbors began to arrive, some of the older, larger, and more traditional grand mansions commissioned by the auto barons as part of the early 20th century industrial boom were starting to disappear. As the original owners began to move or pass away, the realization of the hard work and expense to maintain these larger homes was beginning to become a reality. Many were razed to make way for new subdivisions. According to a 1997 article in the *Detroit News*, "Of the 43 estates listed in a 1956 article about Pointes mansions, only 13 still exist."

The postwar era also saw a dramatic increase in the number of people living in the Grosse Pointe communities. As the population and demographics began to change, so did the number of homes, schools, hospitals, and commercial buildings. Between the mid-1950s and mid-1970s, a new band of architects was hired to create multiple homes across the community, as were local recognized builders who specialized in developing subdivisions within the area.

Time and tide wait for no man, and neither, it would seem, do the constant changes that happen in and around Grosse Pointe.

50 PROVENCAL ROAD. Harrie T. Lindeberg, a nationally recognized architect, designed this home for Ruby Boyer Miller, a wealthy, married socialite. Completed in 1935 in the Greek Revival style, it is situated on a substantial picturesque lot. The home has an abundance of large windows on the rear elevation, while the interior features handsome details throughout. Harrie T. Lindeberg was best known for designing spectacular country houses for prominent families in the United States during the 1910s, 1920s, and 1930s. Each and every one of Lindeberg's creations was finished impeccably, inside and out. The house for Ruby Miller was his one and only project in Grosse Pointe; Miller owned the property for 25 years. The address of this house is now 481 Kercheval Avenue. (Left, courtesy of LOC, LC-G612- 31228 [P&P]; below, LC-G612-31218 [P&P].)

655 LAKE SHORE ROAD. Originally the location of an 18th-century ribbon farm, the property was once home to a large mansion known as Fairlawn. In 1968, Fairlawn was demolished, and a new home was built in 1969. The 7,306-square-foot residence is inspired by architecture found in the Old South. Six large columns dominate the front elevation, as does the 85-foot balcony. (Courtesy of HMA.)

115 LAKE SHORE ROAD. Carl Habermas designed this Mid-Century Modern home in 1953 for the family of auto dealer Stark Hickey. It is partly situated on what was once the location of Drybrook, the Truman Newberry Estate designed by the noted New York City firm of Trowbridge and Ackerman in 1914. In the early 1950s, Drybrook was demolished, and the land subdivided. (Courtesy of HMA.)

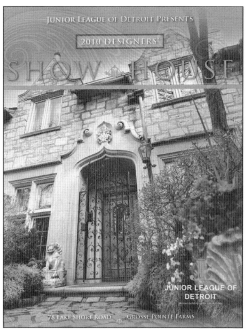

JUNIOR LEAGUE OF DETROIT DESIGNERS' SHOW HOUSE. Since 1976, the Junior League of Detroit has held its Designers' Show House—a biennial event that makes the most of the grand estates in Grosse Pointe. Local and national designers are invited to transform the preselected home into a "show house" for the public to enjoy for several weeks. A Sneak A Peek event is held prior to the main event so members of the public can view the property before it is redesigned. Some properties have required more work than others, and to date, 22 homes have lent themselves to the cause. The occasion, thus far, has raised over $4.5 million for the Junior League of Detroit's community-based projects and programs. (All, courtesy of JLD.)

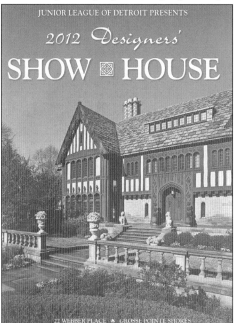

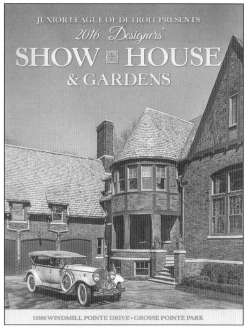

5 AND 12 ALGER PLACE. This new subdivision was created in the 1960s. The land was originally the location of a large residence known as By-Way, designed by William B. Stratton and Frank C. Baldwin. Located at 17700 East Jefferson Avenue, By-Way was completed in 1908 for Frederick Moulton Alger. The residence was demolished in the 1960s, and the land subdivided. Alger Place is made up of 15 homes constructed between 1965 and 1976. Local recognized builder and land developer Richard M. Kimbrough built two of these homes, number 5 and number 12. He specialized in developing subdivisions within Grosse Pointe between the mid-1950s and mid-1970s. Alger Place is just one of the new subdivisions that was built on land once occupied by a grand estate. (Both, courtesy of HMA.)

42 Moross Road. This house is part of the superb collection of Art Deco–inspired Art Moderne homes that were constructed in Grosse Pointe during the 1930s and early 1940s. Frank A. Miles designed 42 Moross Road in 1939, his only home in this style, in the Grosse Pointe communities. (Courtesy of HMA.)

40 Sunningdale Drive. Edmund E. Primeau completed this Colonial home in 1957 for Alfred L. "Budd" Marks and his wife, Virginia Backus. General Marks commanded the 127th Tactical Air Wing at Selfridge Air National Guard Base from around 1955 through 1958. Originally located on a 1.9-acre secluded lot, the house has also been owned by William Clay Ford Jr. and professional baseball player Kirk Gibson, one of Detroit's most famous sporting heroes. (Courtesy of HMA.)

25 Fisher Road. Completed in 1937, this International-style home was created by Hugh T. Keyes for Herbert B. Trix, onetime mayor of Grosse Pointe and president of the American Injector Company. During this phase of his career, Keyes was heavily influenced by functionalism, which is particularly evident in the rounded walls, flat roof, and uniquely curved entranceway of this modern home. (Courtesy of HMA.)

766 Westchester Road. Completed in 1936, this home is an excellent example of the Art Deco style. J.H. Gustav Steffens and Carl R. Habermas designed it for Frank C. Williams. It is constructed from light-colored sandstone and features some exquisite detailing associated with this approach. Art Deco during this era was particularly popular in Detroit, which became home to some of the finest structures in the United States. (Courtesy of HOD.)

LYLE ZISLER, 641 OXFORD ROAD AND 705 PEMBERTON ROAD. Lyle Zisler was a highly skilled architect who was particularly adept at creating Art Deco–inspired homes, along with more formal residences. He was born in 1910 and spent his career in Detroit. Zisler was self-employed and was also the editor for the *Michigan Technic*, an engineering publication published by the University of Michigan. Between 1937 and 1948, Zisler created several homes in the community, including his own home located at 641 Oxford Road in 1937. The Art Moderne–inspired residence is constructed from light-colored sandstone with a low-pitched roof and a two-story glass-block window on the front elevation. That same year, he created 705 Pemberton Road, an Art Deco–inspired, two-story residence that is featured in the book *Art Deco in Detroit*. (Both, courtesy of HMA.)

27 AND 30 HARBOR HILL ROAD. In 1918, John Dodge purchased a large plot of land on Lake Shore Road to build a gigantic mansion. However, after Dodge's unexpected death in 1920, the project was put on hold. In 1925, Matilda Dodge remarried and moved to a property near Rochester, Michigan, that had been purchased by her late husband in 1907. After her departure, the house on Lake Shore Road remained as an empty shell for many years. In 1940, it was dismantled, and the land subdivided to create what is now known as Harbor Hill. From 1950 to 1954, around 20 homes were constructed in numerous architectural styles—Colonial, early American, English, and Ranch. The streets residents now use was once the man-made peninsula that John Dodge had built for his 104-foot power cruiser as a private park. (Both, courtesy of HMA.)

ELIEL AND EERO SAARINEN, 203 CLOVERLY ROAD. The father and son team of Eliel and Eero Saarinen, in conjunction with J. Robert F. Swanson, designed this 5,600-square-foot modern home—their only project in Grosse Pointe. It was completed in 1939 for Charles J. Koebel, owner of the Koebel Diamond Tool Company. Eliel Saarinen was born in Finland in 1873 and immigrated to the United States in 1923. He was already an established architect in Finland. Saarinen initially resided in Evanston, Illinois. In 1924, he became a visiting professor at the University of Michigan. A year later, he was commissioned by George Gough Booth to design the campus of Cranbrook Education Community. It was Booth's intent for Cranbrook to become the American equivalent of the world-famous Bauhaus. Eero Saarinen, born in 1910, was also a highly sought-after designer. Father and son resided and worked in Bloomfield Hills. The residence at 203 Cloverly Road was their first joint commission; Eliel's daughter Pipsan designed the interior of the home, while her husband, J. Robert F. Swanson, created the final plans for the property. (Courtesy of HOD.)

906 Lake Shore Road. During the 1950s, Mid-Century Modern architecture was at its peak of popularity. Completed in 1954, the home at 906 Lake Shore Road was designed by Harold C. Southard for Edythe Fern Melrose, Detroit's "Lady of Charm." The *Detroit News* once reported, "It was the first home to be built for testing all the products before Edythe recommended them on her show." The garden once featured a rare European copper beach tree. (Courtesy of HMA.)

781 Lake Shore Road. In the 1950s and 1960s, several Mid-Century Modern homes appeared on Lake Shore Road. The residence at 781 Lake Shore Road, completed in 1964, is a particularly interesting example of this architectural approach. In 1966, the 3,090-square-foot residence was featured in *Better Homes and Gardens* magazine. The entrance hall is said to be white Italian marble and features a sunken fishpond with Hawaiian volcanic rock and a cascading waterfall. (Courtesy of HMA.)

ALDEN DOW, 741 MIDDLESEX ROAD. Alden B. Dow designed over 70 residences as well as churches, schools, civic centers, and commercial buildings. He once described his organic design philosophy as "Gardens never end and buildings never begin." In Grosse Pointe, he designed only three homes. Alden Dow was born in Midland in 1904 to Herbert Dow, the chemical industrialist and founder of the Dow Chemical Company. Having studied engineering at University of Michigan, he selected to follow a different path and went to study architecture at Columbia University. In 1933, he became an apprentice to Frank Lloyd Wright in the Taliesin Studio. With his training complete, he returned to Midland in 1934 to open his own architecture practice. During this time, he not only built his own home and studio on a 23-acre property, but he also designed and patented "Unit Blocks"—molded masonry units designed to allow strong vertical and horizontal lines. In 1941, he completed the Robbie Robertson House at 741 Middlesex Road. It is one of 13 homes that used the award-winning unit block system. (Courtesy of HOD.)

ALDEN DOW, 888 PEMBERTON ROAD. The first Dow house in Grosse Pointe, at 888 Pemberton Road, was completed in 1936 for Millard Pryor, a wealthy industrialist from Ohio. The 2,659-square-foot International-style residence has a modern open floor plan and features all the classic traits of this approach. Dow specialized in the principles of organic architecture, a similar philosophy to Frank Lloyd Wright. (Courtesy of HOD.)

ALDEN DOW, 96 HANDY ROAD. The Clark T. Wells House was Alden Dow's second project in the community. Built in 1939, the 2,481-square-foot, four-bedroom brick home has superb wood detailing around the exterior and a wood trellis that wraps around two sides of the house. Dow was particularly skilled at basing his designs on the natural environment, a philosophy he maintained throughout his career. (Courtesy of HMA.)

ALEXANDER GIRARD, 222 LOTHROP ROAD. Alexander Girard has been described as one of the most prolific, important, and influential textile designers of the 20th century. He was also a very talented architect and graphic, product, and interior designer. Born in New York City in 1907, he was raised in Florence, Italy, and studied architecture in London and at the Royal School of Architecture in Rome. After returning to the United States, he lived in New York and then relocated to Detroit in 1937. That same year, he opened his first store, located at 16906 Kercheval Avenue, with his business partner H. Beard Adams. They specialized in interior design and architecture. In 1947, the shop was relocated to 379 Fisher Road. During this time, Girard worked on four homes in Grosse Pointe; three are located on Lothrop Road. This includes 234 Lothrop Road and his own home at 222 Lothrop Road, completed in 1948, which he created by combining two smaller houses into one larger residence. In 1953, Girard moved to Santa Fe and worked with a number of high-profile companies, including Herman Miller, Braniff Airways, George Jensen, and John Deere. (Courtesy of HMA.)

ALEXANDER GIRARD, 232 LOTHROP ROAD. Alexander Girard completed this unique home in 1951 for Dr. George Rieveschl, a research chemist. The contemporary residence was located on a secluded wooded ridge of 1.5 acres with over 360 trees, mostly pines and hemlocks. The design featured a 30-foot-by-40-foot atrium and a glass tunnel that connected the main living area to the bedrooms. In 1959, William Kessler extensively remodeled the property. It was razed several years later. (Courtesy of HMA.)

ALEXANDER GIRARD, 55 VENDOME ROAD. Alexander Gerrard completed this unique Mid-Century Modern home, the interior furnishings, and decor for John McLucas in 1950. The rooms in the 4,641-square-foot, one-story structure are grouped around a central courtyard, and the surrounding walls are constructed of glazed bricks in a variety of colors. The house is situated in beautiful surroundings and is barely visible from the road. (Courtesy of HOD.)

William Kessler, 874 Lake Shore Road. One of the most prominent modernist architects to work in Grosse Pointe was William Kessler. Aside from creating 874 Lake Shore Road, he also designed his own home in the community, 1013 Cadieux Road. William Kessler was born in Pennsylvania in 1924. Having served in World War II, Kessler then studied architecture at the Chicago Institute of Design, graduating in 1948. He continued his education at Harvard University under the guidance of Bauhaus School founder Walter Gropius. In 1950, Kessler was living in the Detroit area and was hired by the firm of Minoru Yamasaki as a senior designer. In 1955, he established his own firm with fellow architect Philip Meathe. William Hawkins Ferry, a key figure in championing Detroit architecture and modern architecture, commissioned Kessler to design a new home on Lake Shore Road; it was completed in 1964. The 5,600-square-foot, cube-shaped, two-story modern home is situated on a one-acre lot. Three of the exterior walls are vertical cypress, while the fourth, an east-facing lake-view wall, is glass. Ferry resided in the home until his death in 1988. (Courtesy of HOD.)

LOUIS ROSSETTI, 1145 BALFOUR STREET AND 1119 HARVARD ROAD. Several of Grosse Pointe's noted architects not only created homes in the community, they also resided there. One such designer was Louis Rossetti, master of modern-style homes. He created several homes in the community, including his own at 1145 Balfour Street (above), a five-level house completed in 1940. Born in Paris in 1895, Rossetti served in World War I. Having graduated from Rome University in 1924, he won a scholarship to America. By 1928, he was an established architect in Detroit. That same year he became partner at the firm of Raymond Giffels and Victor Vallet. In the 1950s, the firm of Giffels & Rossetti was one of the largest architectural firms in the country, creating Cobo Hall (now known as the TCF Center) and the Main Terminal Building at the Wayne County Metro Airport in 1958. (Above, courtesy of HOD; below, courtesy of HMA.)

10 PROVENCAL ROAD. Giffels & Vallet, Inc., and Louis Rossetti completed this Streamline Moderne–style residence in 1936. Constructed of concrete, the original design featured a balcony railing, a rounded circular bay, and porthole windows to give it a ship-like appearance, a common trait in homes inspired by the Nautical Deco style—a growing trend in the late 1930s due to the popularity of cruise ships. (Courtesy of HMA.)

15822 LAKEVIEW COURT. Renowned Detroit architect Gino Rossetti completed this modern 2,000-square-foot home in 1977 as his own private residence. Constructed from steel, the design uses cantilevers instead of beams so as not to obstruct the view of the lake, while the exterior is clad in wood. Rossetti, known for his sleek, modern designs, is the son of renowned modernist designer Louis Rossetti, who designed Cobo Hall (now known as the TCF Center). (Courtesy of HMA.)

Six

LOST OVER TIME

Over the years, Grosse Pointe has witnessed the construction of many sublime estates. The community is blessed with an abundance of grand homes, many of which date back to the beginning of the 20th century. However, there have also been a number of large beautiful residences that have been lost over time.

The reasons for razing these properties fall into several categories—estates were sold for subdivision, homes were too big and too costly to maintain, structural problems, fire, or lost because the new homeowner simply wanted to build something else.

It is not just the older estates that have been lost. Some of the newly constructed houses have also been victims of the wrecking ball—modern homes that offered a wonderful contrast to the more formal residences that grace the community.

Work by architectural masters such as Albert Kahn, George D. Mason, Hugh T. Keyes, and Trowbridge and Ackerman have been lost, including grand estates such as Rose Terrace, the Hugo Scherer Mansion, the Truman H. Newberry residence, the Standish Backus Estate, and two modern homes by Alexander Girard.

While these estates are now gone, many have been replaced by new subdivisions such as Sycamore Lane, Stratford Place, Island Lane, and Jefferson Court, to name a few. Countless roads are named in honor of the grand estates or their once prominent owners such as Alger Place, Stephens Lane, and Newberry Place. Other razed homes were replaced with newer construction, while in some cases, elements of the original mansions still exist.

These lost homes typified the opulence that graced Grosse Pointe during the early 20th century and the prominent residents that decided to make Grosse Pointe their home. These homes may have been lost over time, but they are too good to be forgotten.

17000 East Jefferson Avenue. Prominent local architect George W. Graves designed this unique home in 1914 for Oren S. Hawes, an expert in the lumber trade who became associated with a number of lumber companies in Michigan. The style of the house was different to the many large Colonial homes constructed during that era. The home was demolished in the 1970s to make way for what is now Lakeside Court. (Courtesy of HMA.)

507 Lake Shore Road. This sprawling 9,500-square-foot Italian-style villa was completed in 1977 for Pietro (Pete) Gandolfo. The uniquely styled mansion was finished in white stucco with a red tile roof and featured a grand, circular 32-foot front room. The front of the home was dominated by a multitude of arched windows, making the most the lake view. It was demolished in 1998. (Courtesy of HMA.)

241 Lake Shore Road. This magnificent property was completed in 1913, for Sarah Stephens, wife of lumber baron Henry Stephens Jr. Charles A. Platt designed the 25-room French Baroque–style mansion, while noted New York landscape architect William Pitkin Jr. created the gardens. It typified the opulence of the homes that were constructed in the GP Farms during the early 20th century. Prior to its demolition in 1988, an auction was held at the property that attracted bidders from over 1,500 miles away. (Courtesy of HMA.)

735 Lake Shore Road. This Tudor-inspired home was located on a 52-acre estate (20 acres were in Grosse Pointe Woods). Albert Kahn completed it in 1930 for Alvan Macauley, president of Packard Motor Car Company. The estate stretched from Lake Shore Road to the Lochmoor Country Club. At the time, it was arguably one of the largest lots in Grosse Pointe. It was demolished in 1973. (Courtesy of HMA.)

217 LAKE SHORE ROAD. This large modern-styled home, located on a 2.7-acre lot, was completed in 1977 for Edward A. Skoe. Francis Palms Jr. designed it. Many of the main rooms in the property had wonderful views of the lake, thanks to the large glass section on the main floor. The property was demolished between 1992 and 1995. (Courtesy of HMA.)

270 GROSSE POINTE BOULEVARD. This modern mid-century residence was completed in 1961. Karl H. Greimel, a talented designer and former associate of Minoru Yamasaki, an extremely noted architect in the mid-20th century, designed it for Robert L. Gotfredson, vice president of the Trans American Freight Lines Company. A trilevel residence, it was located on a large 1.6-acre lot. It was demolished in 2018. (Courtesy of HMA.)

605 LAKE SHORE ROAD. Built in 1898 for William C. Roney, this house is a good example of an early Dutch Colonial–inspired home—an extremely popular style in Grosse Pointe during the first part of the 20th century. During the 1960s, the residence was described as "probably being of no value." It was subsequently demolished, date unknown, and a new house was built in 1981. (Courtesy of HMA.)

677 LAKE SHORE ROAD. William B. Stratton designed this stunning Italian villa in 1924 for John N. Stalker. The exterior of the house was painted grey stucco, while the rear of the home featured an ornate balcony over a glass-covered porch. It was last sold in 1997 and demolished that same year. A new house was built in 1998. (Courtesy of HMA.)

41 LOCHMOOR BOULEVARD. Completed in 1936 for Lloyd H. Buhs, the secretary-treasurer of the Pfeiffer Brewing Company, this International-style home was designed by prominent local architect Hugh T. Keyes. An innovative design, the exterior featured multiple large windows, a flat roof, and rounded walls. It had a relatively simple floor plan with a large central open space. The two-story, 5,000-square-foot residence was an early foray by Keyes into functionalism—popular in Scandinavia during the 1930s and a favored style of internationally acclaimed architect Le Corbusier. *Architectural Record* magazine described it as "an outstanding example of modern architecture." The Detroit Board of Commerce sponsored the project as a "Made in Detroit" home, which meant it was equipped and built with materials made in Detroit. Hugh T. Keyes went on to adapt the International style into his own Regency Moderne style—a popular approach for much of his work from the 1930s onward. The residence at 41 Lochmoor Boulevard was demolished during the 1990s. (Courtesy of HMA.)

17800 EAST JEFFERSON AVENUE. Albert Kahn designed this English Manor–inspired residence in 1905 for Charles M. Swift, a lawyer who made his fortune in mining. Having practiced law until around 1893, Swift then turned his attention to building and operating electric trams and railroads in Michigan and the Philippines. The house was demolished in the 1980s. (Courtesy of LOC, LC-D4-62781 [P&P].)

17040 EAST JEFFERSON AVENUE. This was the first of three residences designed by the New York firm of Trowbridge and Ackerman. Known as Elmsleigh, it was commissioned by Luther S. Trowbridge, a lawyer, businessman, and brother of the architect. Completed in 1909, this home's style is a loose interpretation of English Domestic Revival. It was demolished during the 1960s, and the land subdivided to create Lakeside Court, next to Elmsleigh Lane. (Courtesy of HMA.)

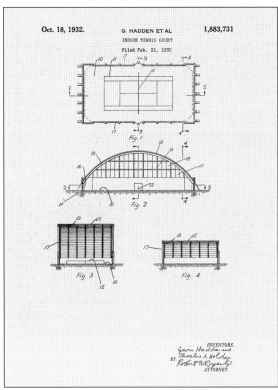

Oct. 18, 1932.   G. HADDEN ET AL   1,883,731

INDOOR TENNIS COURT

Filed Feb. 21, 1930

Fig.1

Fig.2

Fig. 3

Fig. 4

INVENTORS.
Gavin Hadden and
Charles A. Holden
BY Robert A Byerly
ATTORNEY

THE TENNIS HOUSE, PATENT AND EXTERIOR. Members of the Ford family commissioned the Tennis House, located at 360 Moselle Place in GP Farms. It opened for play in January 1936 as a private indoor tennis club. The structure, which housed one court, was designed by New York–based architect and engineer Gavin Hadden. Having graduated from Harvard University in 1910 and served in Europe during World War I, he opened his own engineering office. Hadden helped design several large sports stadiums, such as the Philadelphia Stadium and Brown University Stadium. In the late 1920s, Hadden created a design for an indoor tennis house building. In 1930, he filed a patent application in conjunction with Charles A. Holden. It was officially patented in 1932. It was this design that the Tennis House is based on. (Left, courtesy of Google Patents; below, courtesy of the Kornmeier family.)

THE TENNIS HOUSE, PLAYERS' LOUNGE AND COURT. The private club was open for around 80 years and was limited to 100 members. For many years, there was a waiting list to join. It was only open during the winter, and reservations were required to play on the single clay court. The weekends were reserved for men only. The building was constructed from glass and steel with a wood roof. It also had the first gas-fired steam boiler in the area. The Art Deco–inspired interior featured a small kitchen and bar, male and female locker rooms, and a lobby. It is not known how many of these structures (by Gavin Hadden) were built or how many still exist in the United States. Around 2016, it was no longer feasible to run the Tennis House as a private club. As a result of structural issues, it was demolished in 2019. (Both, courtesy of the Kornmeier family.)

665 LAKE SHORE ROAD. Hugh T. Keyes completed this Regency Moderne home in 1951 for Robert Pauli Scherer, who made his fortune with the invention of the rotary die encapsulation process to encapsulate medicines. The 7,050-square-foot home, located on three lots, overlooked the lake and included a fully equipped metalworking and woodworking shop. It was demolished around 2010, and the large lot was subdivided. (Courtesy of HMA.)

70 LAKE SHORE DRIVE. This striking English Tudor–inspired home was built in 1910 for H. Chalmers. The rear of the home overlooked Lake St. Clair and had a 297-foot seawall. It was enlarged in 1921, last sold in 1995, and demolished in the late 1990s. (Courtesy of HMA.)

70 Moran Road. William F. Goodrich completed 70 Moran Road, also known as Sunnycroft, in 1919 for Cornelia Anderson, widow of William K. Anderson, the former manager of the Detroit Seed Co. and a director of several companies owned by the Newberry-McMillan Corporation. The house was created in the English Cottage style. The formal garden was particularly impressive; an upper terrace at the front of the residence featured an abundance of large trees, while a more formal lower terrace—with a pond, well-kept borders, and beautiful lawns—created a stunning landscape at the rear of the home. The garden is an excellent example of some of the large, beautiful gardens that could be found throughout Grosse Pointe during that era. It appears 70 Moran Road was partly demolished in 1946, followed by complete demolition in 1957. It is now the location of Moran Court. Many of the large trees still exist from the estate between the area of Moran Road and the adjacent part of Merriweather Road. (Courtesy of HMA.)

66 RENAUD ROAD. George D. Mason & Company completed this Colonial home in 1938 for Robert A. Foster. With a career spanning over 50 years, this was one of Mason's final projects in the community. He died in 1948. Over a period of 56 years, he created many beautiful homes in Grosse Pointe, many of which still exist. The original home at 66 Renaud Road was demolished in the early 2000s, and a new home was built. (Courtesy of HMA.)

99 LAKE SHORE DRIVE. Earnest Wilby, of Albert Kahn Associates, designed the Georgian-inspired John S. Newberry Estate, called Lake Terrace, in 1911. Ellen Biddle Shipman designed the formal gardens. The gardens proved the perfect setting for parties and events, while the greenhouse was always filled with azaleas and cyclamens. Upon Edith Newberry's death in 1956, the home was deemed too costly to maintain. It was demolished in 1957, and the land was subdivided. It is now the location of Warner Road. (Courtesy of LOC, LC-J717-X110-128 [P&P].)

431 LAKE SHORE ROAD. The William P. Stevens residence was a magnificent Georgian-inspired home located on a large lot, only accessible from Kercheval Avenue. Smith, Hinchman & Grylls completed it in 1914 for William Stevens, a real estate developer specializing in industrial centers, predominantly Highland Park. The front of the home, facing the lake, was particularly striking, while the rear of the home was more reserved in its appearance. The house underwent extensive alterations in 1929 by noted Grosse Pointe architect Hugh T. Keyes, which changed the symmetry of the original design. One of Keyes's specialties was making wide-scale changes to older homes to bring them more in-line with how families wanted to live in the late 1920s and early 1930s. He completed multiple projects of this kind. In 1984, the house was demolished due to structural problems and maintenance issues. (Courtesy of HMA.)

111 LAKE SHORE ROAD. This 15,000-square-foot Tudor Revival home, known as Cherryhurst, was completed in 1907 for Paul H. Deming, an engineer and banker. It was one of the first year-round residences to be built in GP Farms. In 1996, the home was listed in the National Register of Historic Places and became a designated Michigan State Historic Site. Yet despite the historical recognition, it was demolished in 1997 and the land subdivided. (Courtesy of HMA.)

1000 LAKE SHORE ROAD. The grand Georgian-style residence of Louis Mendelssohn was completed in 1928; it is not clear who the architect was. Mendelssohn served as chairman of the board of the Fisher Body Corporation. The home was decorated throughout with teakwood paneled walls in the dining room, while seven maids' bedrooms were located on the third floor. It was demolished around 1959, and a new house was built in its place. (Courtesy of HMA.)

15600 WINDMILL POINTE. J. Ivan Dise designed the large English Manor house in 1929 for John W. Drake, former president of Hupp Motor Car and one of the four original investors of the company. Located on a triple lot, the residence featured a grand two-story 23-by-40-square-foot living room with a cathedral ceiling, a 17-by-26-square-foot wood paneled library, a 17-by-23-square-foot dining room, a 21-by-40-square-foot solarium, and an adjoining slate terrace overlooking the lake. Prior to 1970, the house was purchased by another key figure in the automotive industry, Carl Breer. Along with Fred Zeder and Owen Skelton, Breer was one of the key engineers that formed the present-day Chrysler Corporation. Breer passed in 1970 and was inducted into the Automotive Hall of Fame in 1976. In the mid-1990s, the house was badly damaged by fire and was subsequently demolished. (Courtesy of HMA.)

DISCOVER THOUSANDS OF LOCAL HISTORY BOOKS FEATURING MILLIONS OF VINTAGE IMAGES

Arcadia Publishing, the leading local history publisher in the United States, is committed to making history accessible and meaningful through publishing books that celebrate and preserve the heritage of America's people and places.

Find more books like this at
www.arcadiapublishing.com

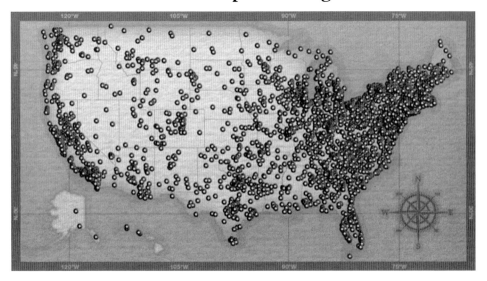

Search for your hometown history, your old stomping grounds, and even your favorite sports team.

Consistent with our mission to preserve history on a local level, this book was printed in South Carolina on American-made paper and manufactured entirely in the United States. Products carrying the accredited Forest Stewardship Council (FSC) label are printed on 100 percent FSC-certified paper.

MADE IN THE USA